Having recently read the book I found ... [illegible]
The book provided me with both theoretical and practical knowledge about the technology, and I believe it would be beneficial to a diverse range of audiences, including those in computer science, business, accountancy, and economics.

Dr Andrew Bingham, Dean, Teesside University
International Business School

Getting Started with Cryptocurrency is an excellent primer which uses clear and accessible language to explain many of the key concepts behind cryptocurrency and blockchain. Providing answers to all of the most frequently asked questions about these technologies, author Kate Baucherel delves into where cryptocurrency came from as well as providing insights into how it is being used in the real world now and hints at what a tokenised future may look like. An invaluable resource.

Helen Disney, CEO, Unblocked

This beginner-friendly book is an exhilarating read; demystifies digital assets, whilst offering clear insights and practical tips for a seamless entry into the crypto universe. Highly recommended.

Chikezie Ekeanyanwu FRSA FRAI, Chair, BCS FINSIG

This book helps demystify the complexities of cryptocurrency, and Kate skilfully navigates the reader through both the dazzling allure and the intricate subtleties of cryptocurrencies, crafting a narrative that captivates both seasoned insiders and curious newcomers alike. Even as a veteran in the crypto world, I found new insights and knowledge within its pages.

Genevieve Leveille, CEO and Founder, AgriLedger

An excellent primer for business leaders looking to innovate and engage new customers. This book sheds light on the role of digital assets and crypto infrastructure in the digital economy. Baucherel does more for mainstreaming crypto with this book than all the NFT projects ever launched. This comprehensive take on crypto, from fundamentals to future-shock, offers a solid roadmap for innovators interested in blockchain for growth.

Fiona Delaney, Blockchain Strategic Lead, SEEBLOCKS.eu
and Founder, Origin Chain Networks

An impressive read. Well structured, clear and easy to read. A must for experienced traders as well as someone buying their very first cryptocurrency. I will be buying copies for my employees to make sure that they all have a firm grasp of the subject matter!

Antony Abell, CEO & Founder of the TPX™ Property Exchanges

Getting Started with Cryptocurrency is a must-have book for early explorers and seasoned professionals alike. The author covers a broad range of complex and rapidly evolving topics in a well-ordered and approachable manner, with clear takeaways to help newcomers avoid pitfalls. This is not written for the get-rich-quick crowd, but for those who have been turned off by the tech speak and others who want to get up to date with the state of the art. I can easily recommend this book to anyone interested in this field.

Dr Robert M. Learney, Head of Distributed Systems, Digital Catapult

Getting Started with Cryptocurrency is a gem in the crypto literature landscape. As a pioneer in the field, I found myself pleasantly surprised by the wealth of knowledge it offered, even to someone well-versed in the space. This book's clear and concise writing style makes it accessible to both newbies and seasoned veterans alike. It's become a staple on my bookshelf, and I'll be gifting copies to family and friends eager for advice and understanding. Consider the solution found!

Morten Rongaard, Co-Konungr Viking, PixelPai

GETTING STARTED WITH CRYPTOCURRENCY

An introduction to digital assets and blockchain

Kate Baucherel

bcs
The Chartered Institute for IT

Contents

List of Figures

About the Author

Kate Baucherel is an author, speaker and emerging technology consultant specialising in blockchain and cryptocurrency. She works with clients from start-up and scale-up businesses to blue chip multinationals. Over a career spanning more than 35 years, she has held senior technical and financial roles in sectors including utilities, construction, manufacturing, leisure and software, leading several enterprises through their start-up and growth phases.

Kate graduated in business from Newcastle University and is a Fellow of the Chartered Institute of Management Accountants. She teaches Masters courses in fintech, blockchain and digital transformation at Teesside University, speaks at conferences around the world and appears regularly on the BBC. Her books include *Blockchain Hurricane* (BEP/Harvard 2020) and the SimCavalier cybercrime thrillers.

Acknowledgements

This book would not have been possible without the vision and guidance of the BCS publishing team. Thank you for the opportunity to dig deeper into a subject I love and bring it to a wider audience.

I have been involved in the ever-changing world of blockchain and crypto assets since 2015, and it has been quite a journey. The crypto community is enthusiastic, collaborative and supportive, and truly global. I'd like to acknowledge all of my friends, colleagues and connections in the industry that I have met and worked with over the years from the UK, USA, Europe, Africa, South-East Asia and Latin America, and who are too numerous to list here.

I've gathered some very specific insights for this book from crypto legacy specialist Richard Marshall, fine artist James Atkins and friends in The Digital Commonwealth, The Bigger Pie, House of Block, and other groups who have answered mysterious questions and resolved arguments about sticky technical points during the creative process.

I'm also ever grateful for the patience of my husband and daughters who keep the world turning while I am deep in research.

1   Crypto: Scam or Opportunity?

Crypto assets are one of the most interesting yet divisive technologies to emerge from the last 15 years of accelerating digital innovation. Different types of crypto assets and blockchains are used in virtually every business sector from supply chains to construction, from banking to luxury goods, in retail, sport, art and gaming. Central banks across the world are testing or already using crypto technology to create digital versions of their national currencies. According to We Are Social's *Digital 2024* global overview (2024), 9.7% of adults globally hold crypto assets. It is likely that some of your clients, customers, suppliers, employees or family members are among them.

This book gives you an overview of different crypto assets, the blockchains beneath them, the ways that they improve processes, transform lives, and create new economic and business models, and the risks associated with them (see Figure 1.1). We outline best practices for managing and securing crypto assets and examine the evolving regulatory landscape. We consider the questions that should be asked to protect individuals and businesses. We'll also take a deeper dive into the technology under the hood, developing a greater understanding of the nuts and bolts to help you make informed decisions around the use of blockchain and crypto.

Figure 1.1 Getting started with crypto and blockchain

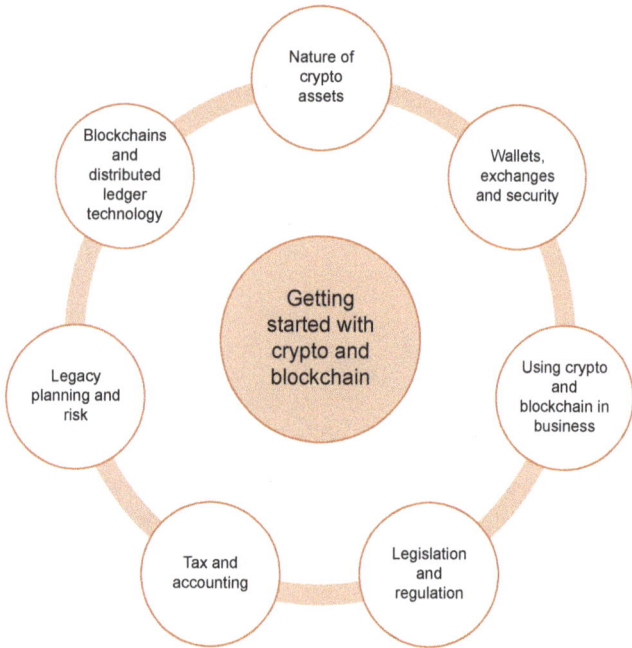

Nature of crypto assets

Blockchains and distributed ledger technology

Wallets, exchanges and security

Getting started with crypto and blockchain

Legacy planning and risk

Using crypto and blockchain in business

Tax and accounting

Legislation and regulation

Cryptocurrency, digital asset, crypto asset, token, or simply crypto?

Throughout this book, the umbrella term **crypto asset** is used unless a specific description is more appropriate. **Crypto** is occasionally used to encompass the assets, the industry and the technology. There is no firm agreement on a standard definition as we can see below, but crypto asset (one word or two, derived from 'cryptographic asset') is the most commonly used.

HMRC uses 'Cryptoassets (also referred to as "tokens" or "cryptocurrency")' in its tax guidance (HMRC, 2024a).

According to a House of Commons briefing on the regulation of cryptocurrency (Browning and Codd, 2023), '"Cryptocurrency" is the more familiar term for a major sub-group of what the Government and regulators prefer to call "cryptoassets"'. The Law Commission uses the term 'digital assets (including crypto-tokens and cryptoassets)' (Law Commission, 2023). The Financial Conduct Authority (FCA) refers simply to 'crypto' in its InvestSmart guidance (2024), explaining that 'Crypto can be thought of as "digital representations of value or rights" that are secured by encryption and typically use some type of "distributed ledger technology" (DLT)'. In its regulatory guidance, however, the FCA refers to 'cryptoassets' and subdivides them into different types of token (FCA, 2023). In the United States, the Securities and Exchange Commission (SEC) talks about crypto assets, while the Commodity Futures Trading Commission (CFTC) prefers digital assets, crypto and virtual currencies (CFTC, 2024). We will look at the nuances of different terms in Chapter 2.

WHERE DID CRYPTO ASSETS COME FROM?

Crypto assets started life as an idea in a paper entitled 'Bitcoin: A Peer-to-Peer Electronic Cash System'. This was published on 31 October 2008 by an unknown author or authors using the pseudonym Satoshi Nakamoto (2008). The first block of the Bitcoin blockchain was created on 3 January 2009. The automated system that underpins Bitcoin, the Bitcoin blockchain, provides an independent, transparent and trusted ledger of every Bitcoin transaction. It is decentralised, in other words not under the control of any single entity, and has been running steadily since its creation, facilitating transactions and gradually increasing the circulating supply of Bitcoins on a pre-programmed schedule.

Who is Satoshi Nakamoto?

There is plenty of speculation, but nobody knows for sure. The pseudonym may represent more than one person, and it's likely that one of the parties is British, another possibly Estonian. They may have subscribed to the Crypto Anarchist Manifesto (May, 1988) that talks of cryptography altering 'government interference in economic transactions' and property rights, and were almost certainly part of the later Cypherpunk movement.

Nakamoto's innovation gave us an honest ledger of transactions, showing the creation and movement of Bitcoins in an automated ledger made up of timestamped blocks. We will look at the structure and functions of a blockchain in more detail in Chapter 7 and explain how it achieves the properties of trust, transparency and decentralisation.

The idea of Bitcoin gradually gained traction beyond the immediate tech community. It accrued a real-world value as Bitcoins changed hands between early adopters and sharp-eyed investors and was first used as a means of payment for goods in 2010, when a pizza was bought for 10,000 Bitcoin. Other crypto assets were created on new blockchains; one or two at first and then, as the hype grew and values rose, hundreds emerged in a gold rush of development. Bitcoin (commonly abbreviated to BTC) was closely followed by others, including Litecoin in 2011, Dogecoin in 2013 and Ethereum (ETH) in 2015. These became known as cryptocurrencies. According to Statista (2024), in 2023 there were just over 9,000 cryptocurrencies in circulation, although the top 20 accounted for more than 90% of the market.

All crypto assets have four things in common:

- They are cryptographically secured and cannot be duplicated or copied.

- They are programmable, interacting with software applications.

- They are owned, conferring rights on the holder to use and dispose of them.

- Their entire transaction history is recorded on a distributed ledger.

A WORLD OF OPPORTUNITIES

The potential of blockchain's uniquely structured and trusted ledgers and the mechanisms of peer-to-peer asset transfers caught the imagination of innovative businesses very quickly. We will look in detail at some of the applications of crypto assets and blockchain in Chapter 4. It's possible that things in your daily life have already been touched by this technology. Here are just a few examples of the way that blockchain and crypto are already being used:

- Payments across borders may well have used underlying crypto technology within the banks' systems to exchange between two currencies.

- Food crops are being traced from farm to table, providing evidence of source and sustainability and helping small producers to access trade finance.

- Electric vehicle manufacturers are using blockchain to establish transparent records of their entire supply chain from ore to battery, and improve conditions and emissions at every stage.

- Global shipping relies on distributed ledger technology to manage and adjust insurance premiums in real time.

- Luxury goods can be verified as genuine through blockchain records, discouraging counterfeiters.

- Fan communities are reaping loyalty rewards and engaging with their favourite sports teams through ownership of club tokens.

- Philanthropic causes are raising money and distributing it to those in need through community voting in distributed autonomous organisations.

- Creators of digital fine art can sell their work without converting it to physical media.

- Construction projects are recording design changes on a trusted and verifiable ledger in line with recommendations made following the Grenfell fire.

POLICE AND THIEVES

Wherever there is value, there are criminals. Headlines about hacks and fraud in crypto asset trading and investment often disguise the exciting opportunities offered by crypto assets and by the underlying technology of blockchain. It's useful to examine why crypto assets attract criminal activity and put some of the high-profile news headlines into context.

The crypto anarchist philosophy behind the creation of Bitcoin was to find a way to make payments without using central banks or other intermediaries. This use-case of circumventing authority suits criminals. Gangs stopped asking for ransomware payments in dollars and started asking for Bitcoin. Crypto allowed them to transact easily and often untraceably on dark web marketplaces and it continues to be a popular medium of exchange and store of value for criminals.

The first high-profile failure of a crypto platform came in 2014, when exchange Mt. Gox collapsed thanks to three years of varied and sustained attacks that manipulated pricing and drained its resources (MIT Technology Review, 2019). Subsequent and frequent cyber-attacks on other crypto platforms have used social engineering, trojans and malware to gain access to ownership credentials, or have targeted weaknesses in the way individual blockchains and their functions are coded.

> What happened to Mt. Gox? A combination of keylogging malware collecting login credentials, unencrypted keys granting access to customer funds and flaws in the source code allowed cybercriminals to drain 850,000 Bitcoin from the exchange from around 2011 to its collapse in 2014. 200,000 Bitcoin have since been recovered.

One of the largest of these was the 2022 theft of $625 million of assets from the bridge between gaming blockchain Ronin and the Ethereum network, where attackers gained control of the mechanism that secured transactions on the bridge.

Assets that have been stolen can be traced through the blockchain ledgers, and while it can be challenging to recover them – for example, two thirds of the assets stolen from Ronin have been traced to the Lazarus cybercrime group in North Korea – forensics and law enforcement agencies are increasingly successful in making seizures and arrests (Plante, 2022).

As the price of Bitcoin rose and the early adopters found themselves with a surprise windfall, frauds and scams followed. Fraudsters issued their own digital money, promising naïve investors pots of gold at the end of a new rainbow, then sank without trace or redress. Others promised high returns on deposits but vanished with their customers' assets. In a report for Bloomberg (Dowlat, 2018), researchers from Satis Group examined all the new crypto assets released to investors in 2017. Seventy-eight per cent of these were found to be scams, although the researchers noted of the approximately $12 billion raised, 90% went to legitimate projects. To put this sum into context, 2017 saw global venture capital investment into traditional start-ups hit a record high at the time of $155 billion (KPMG, 2018) and research indicates that as many as 75% of VC-backed business do not provide a return, with around a third failing entirely (Pollman, 2023).

> Do employers have a duty of care towards their staff to help them spot frauds and scams?
>
> Criminals are clever. Crypto scams often rely on social engineering, using networks of friends and work and religious communities to entice unwary people into the net and part them from their money. Coscoin, a fraudulent cryptocurrency trading platform, used network marketing on messaging apps to build a Ponzi scheme promising great returns. Its collapse in 2023, three months after a warning from the Washington State Department of Financial Institutions, left a group of employees of Nissan in Sunderland without their investments.

In November 2022, the collapse of the FTX crypto exchange and the Alameda Research Group shook the crypto industry. Former CEO Sam Bankman-Fried was found guilty of fraud and money laundering a year later. By that time, thanks to the traceability of crypto assets, $7.3 billion, around 85% of the $8.7 billion of missing assets had been recovered.

FTX became known as 'Crypto's Lehman moment' but it is worth reflecting that when the Lehman Brothers filed for bankruptcy in September 2008, they were $613 billion in debt. $115 billion was paid out in the final liquidation in September 2022 (Stempel, 2022). The speed and scale of asset recovery from the FTX collapse was impressive by comparison, and the final losses were less than 0.3% of those suffered by Lehman's creditors.

However, lessons must be learned from FTX. There was a lack of corporate governance and oversight that would not be expected in a traditional industry start-up. The rapid growth and high value of FTX was based on a crypto asset they had created, FTT. The scam followed the classic pattern of tempting people with too-good-to-be-true returns, then using the funds that customers deposited to pay debts and make up trading shortfalls for other companies in the group and to fund a lavish lifestyle.

Law enforcement agencies are fast catching up with criminals who choose to take advantage of crypto. Transparent blockchain ledgers enable forensic analysis of the movement of stolen assets and proceeds of crime. Assets are being recovered and successful prosecutions brought. Regulation and legislation are being developed and enacted in multiple jurisdictions to protect consumers while trying to still encourage genuine innovation. We will look at these in more detail in Chapter 5.

THE QUESTION OF ENERGY

Blockchain is unfairly associated with heavy energy consumption. This is rather like suggesting that all trains are slow and run on coal like the original Stephenson's Rocket. In this case, the Bitcoin blockchain is the slow, energy-hungry, yet transformative innovation, and modern blockchains are faster and cleaner.

Energy use is baked into the original design of Bitcoin. The mechanism for securing the blockchain and creating new coins, known as Proof of Work, specifically requires the use of electricity. 'The steady addition of a constant amount of new coins is analogous to gold miners expending resources to add gold to circulation,' says Nakamoto. 'In our case, it is CPU time and electricity that is expended.'

Bitcoin mining has struggled to shed its poor reputation. When Kazakhstan welcomed mining operations in 2017 to make use of excess energy, it seemed to be a good economic decision for the country. By 2022, the industry was draining the country's resources, and was banned (Guest, 2023).

When Bitcoin's network was being secured by a handful of tech enthusiasts using their laptops and home computers to 'mine' the asset with their CPU time and electricity, this was not of great concern. As the demand for Bitcoin rose, specialised mining operations sprang up, running processors day and night to win a share of the new coins being added to the supply. These turned into a global industry, with shipping containers full of processors drawing energy primarily from fossil fuel sources. In 2021 when the price of Bitcoin rose to over $76,000, researchers at Digiconomist estimated that the Bitcoin blockchain was consuming electricity at an annual rate of 200 TWh.

Figure 1.2 Bitcoin energy consumption 2017–2023 (The Bitcoin Energy Consumption index is developed and maintained by Alex de Vries at www.digiconomist.net, and is reproduced here with his permission.)

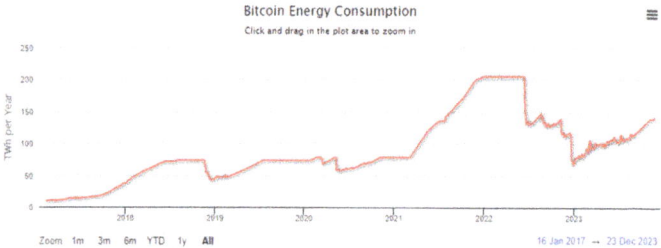

But the industry has moved on. Modern blockchains have developed a range of much faster, cleaner mechanisms that do not require constant energy-hungry processing to secure the chain. Other than Bitcoin, only a handful of small older blockchains use the Proof of Work mechanism. Renewable, nuclear and geothermal energy sources are being tapped by responsible miners. Cornell University researchers suggest renewable energy projects could be funded by mining in the pre-commercial phase when they are generating electricity but not sending to the grid (Lal, Zhu and You, 2023).

In September 2022, Ethereum, the second largest blockchain, successfully changed its security and supply mechanism to Proof of Stake, using passive voting rather than active competition to confirm blocks. In doing so it reduced its power demand by at least 99.84%, a saving equivalent to the energy required to power Austria. Perhaps Ethereum's success in changing its software will point the way for Bitcoin to do the same (de Vries, 2023).

Figure 1.3 Ethereum change in energy consumption at adoption of Proof of Stake (The Ethereum Energy Consumption index is developed and maintained by Alex de Vries at www.digiconomist.net, and is reproduced here with his permission)

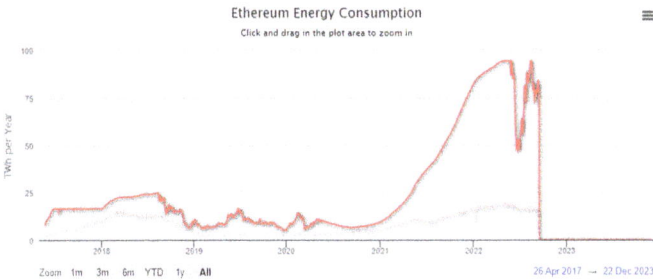

Ironically, defunct Ethereum processors and unprofitable Bitcoin mines are turning to the opportunities offered by another new technology. According to research published by JP Morgan (CryptoCurrencyWire, 2023), 'mining companies are branching into fresh business domains, diversifying into high-performance computing services for the rapidly expanding artificial intelligence sector'. Our appetite for energy-consuming technologies is only increasing.

DECODING CRYPTO ASSETS

The complex jargon of crypto is one of the main barriers to adoption. What's the difference between a crypto asset and a cryptocurrency or a token? What's meant by a wallet, a key, or an exchange? What is an NFT, and why should we care?

In the next chapter, we will decode the jargon and explore what you can do with different types of crypto asset.

Chapter 1 Key takeaways

- Crypto assets are programmable and ownable things.

- A blockchain records the movement of crypto assets on a trusted and transparent ledger.

- Where there is money, there are criminals. If it looks too good to be true, it probably is.

- Your family, friends and employees may already be using crypto. Are they doing it safely?

- Crypto assets other than Bitcoin use very little energy to run, and all technology is energy dependent.

2 The Language and Landscape of Crypto

Understanding the language of crypto opens the door to informed use of the technology and an appreciation of the legislation that surrounds crypto activities. Unfortunately, there is a lot of jargon to cut through. In this chapter we will look at the different types of crypto asset and the actions that can be taken with these assets – acquiring them, using them and keeping them secure.

Figure 2.1 The crypto asset family tree

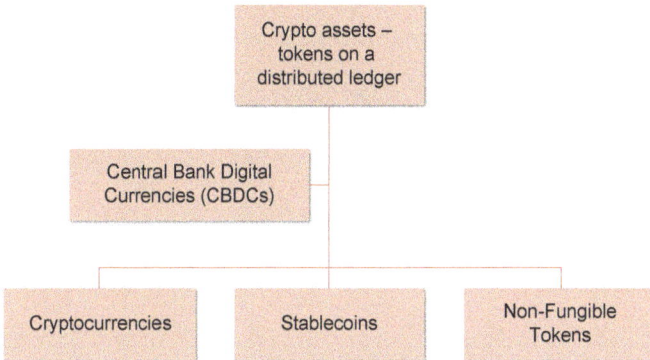

```
              ┌──────────────────────┐
              │   Crypto assets –    │
              │     tokens on a      │
              │  distributed ledger  │
              └──────────┬───────────┘
                         │
        ┌────────────────┤
┌───────┴──────────┐     │
│ Central Bank     │     │
│ Digital          │     │
│ Currencies       │     │
│ (CBDCs)          │     │
└──────────────────┘     │
                         │
      ┌──────────────────┼──────────────────┐
┌─────┴─────────┐ ┌──────┴──────┐ ┌─────────┴──────┐
│Cryptocurrencies│ │ Stablecoins │ │  Non-Fungible  │
│               │ │             │ │     Tokens     │
└───────────────┘ └─────────────┘ └────────────────┘
```

CRYPTO ASSET, DIGITAL ASSET OR TOKEN?

As we saw in Chapter 1, different terms to describe crypto assets are being used more or less interchangeably among legislators, regulators, financial bodies, businesses and consumers. However, it is important to understand the nuances of each term as they may be used to distinguish between certain assets.

At the most basic level, all crypto assets are tokens. Token is a generic term for an algorithmic data object, a discrete item of code that's programmed to work within a software application. For example, in artificial intelligence, tokens are the basic units of text that a large language model like ChatGPT uses to generate language.

In crypto, tokens can represent ownership, value and information. Their movements are recorded on their blockchain, and they are programmed to perform specific actions when interacting with the software applications on their blockchain. An ETH token is part of the software that executes a transaction on the Ethereum network. An XRP token is programmed to play the 'joker' in a traditional foreign exchange transaction on the Ripple blockchain, forming a bridge between two currencies. A LINK token manages the transfer of data from a trusted source, an Oracle, on the Chainlink blockchain.

Utility and security tokens

These descriptions hit the headlines in legal cases, particularly in the United States where laws around investment are much stricter than in other jurisdictions. Where tokens have been sold on cryptocurrency markets to raise funds before or during the development of a blockchain project, businesses have to show that their token has 'utility', which means it is essential to the functioning of the software under development, rather than being a 'security' that has been sold like stocks and shares without giving the investor due protection. Tokens judged to be securities fall foul of Securities and Exchange Commission (SEC) regulations.

Terms used for individual tokens may distinguish between their natures and functions or reflect the taxonomic preference of an individual or organisation. We might refer to crypto assets or digital assets, utility tokens or security tokens, cryptocurrencies, altcoins, stablecoins, CBDCs or NFTs depending on their features, their usage, or their classification under securities legislation.

CRYPTOCURRENCIES

Cryptocurrency refers to a crypto asset that mimics the properties of money. In legal and tax terms, with a few notable exceptions around the world, cryptocurrency is not considered to be money or legal tender. However, some cryptocurrencies fulfil the key criteria to be money, in particular Bitcoin (Mattke, Maier and Reis, 2020) which is a liquid asset, a medium of exchange, a store of value and a unit of account. Bitcoin was such a groundbreaking innovation that cryptocurrencies other than Bitcoin are sometimes referred to as 'altcoins', an alternative to Bitcoin.

Liquidity

Bitcoin and Ethereum have a high volume of transactions and strong demand and supply. They are commodities that can be converted rapidly into goods, services or other assets. In other words, they have high liquidity.

Cryptocurrencies outside the top echelons, probably the majority of the 9,000 identified by Statista (see Chapter 1), have much lower activity and may not be easily converted or sold.

A medium of exchange

Money is exchangeable against goods and services. Bitcoin was first used to buy a real-world asset in May 2010, when Laszlo Hanyecz exchanged 10,000 of them, worth around $40 at the time, for two pizzas (Kamsky, 2023). In 2017, real estate platform Propy enabled the first purchase of a house using

Ethereum. Cryptocurrencies can be used to buy any goods and services in the real or virtual world as long as the buyer and seller agree on the transaction. This is particularly useful for cross-border payments, as cryptocurrency transactions have immediate settlement and can be cheaper than traditional bank transfers.

Store of value

The idea of volatile cryptocurrencies being a store of value seems counterintuitive. Empirical studies carried out by Mattke, Maier and Reis (2020) suggest that Bitcoin's limited supply – there will only ever be 21 million Bitcoin – give it the long-term stability needed to be considered as a store of value, and it has been compared to gold as a safe haven for investors (Rashid, Bakry and Al-Mohamad, 2023). In countries where the local currency is more volatile than crypto, there is less of a debate. In Venezuela, using Bitcoin to preserve value in the face of rampant inflation has been a popular strategy among individuals with the knowledge to access the network (Baucherel, 2020).

The volatility of Bitcoin sparked the emergence of a special subset of cryptocurrencies – stablecoins.

STABLECOINS

Stablecoins are a special class of crypto asset. They mitigate the fluctuations of traditional cryptocurrencies while retaining the ability to make low-cost instant payments through a public ledger. The Financial Stability Board (FSB) considers that the stabilisation mechanism distinguishes stablecoins from other cryptocurrencies (FSB, 2023). Tether was the first stablecoin, issued in 2014 and pegged to the value of the US Dollar (USD). Others have followed, pegged not only to the dollar but to other fiat currencies, and even commodities such as gold or crude oil, although commodity-backed coins have lower liquidity.

Stablecoins have attracted concern and criticism around their security and their use (Adachi et al., 2022). Research has drawn attention to the relationship between Tether and Bitcoin activity, raising suspicions of price manipulation (Grobys & Huynh, 2022). The catastrophic crash of the Terra stablecoin in May 2022 revealed that its stabilisation mechanism relied on the market capitalisation of a related cryptocurrency, Luna. When both the crypto and stock markets fell due to global macroeconomic factors including the invasion of Ukraine, the value of Luna could not be maintained, and Terra duly collapsed. In November 2023 the European Banking Authority set out proposals to ensure that issuers of stablecoins hold sufficient funds to fully redeem investors (Jones, 2023).

The proliferation of stablecoins, and proposals by major corporations to issue their own currencies, focused the attention of the world's central banks on crypto technology. The Libra concept proposed by Facebook in July 2018 and later abandoned (Murphy & Stacey, 2022) raised the possibility of two billion Facebook users having access to a common currency and bringing with it a potential threat to national monetary stability. In August 2023, PayPal launched a USD-pegged stablecoin.

In a speech in October 2023, François Villeroy de Galhau, Governor of Banque de France, said, 'Paypal's project of a global stablecoin for retail payments is a stark reminder that if we don't take the initiative, someone else will' (Banque de France, 2023). If any organisation is in a position to issue a stablecoin, it is a bank.

CENTRAL BANK DIGITAL CURRENCIES (CBDCS)

There is a difference between central bank money and the money in a business or personal bank account. Consumers and businesses use the apps supplied by commercial banks and financial institutions to transact with their institution's money. The only central bank money that the public touches is paper bank notes. The idea of digital central bank money is attractive, and crypto technology is at the core of their development. As CBDCs are under the control of a bank rather than decentralised, they are not strictly cryptocurrency, but they are a token and considered to be a form of digital asset.

Cross-border payments are a priority of the G20, with the target that by 2030 credits should reach the recipient's account within one hour. Swift payments already achieve a speed of less than an hour bank to bank, but only 80% of transactions in Europe and 25–30% elsewhere in the world reach the account holders in that time. CBDCs could be the solution to reduce friction and speed up wholesale transactions between countries. European central banks are working together to develop a Euro stablecoin, with live transaction trials planned for 2024.

According to the Atlantic Council (2023), more than 100 countries around the world are exploring CBDCs and 30 have been piloted or launched. Among these, Project Bridge trialled wholesale CBDC transactions between Hong Kong, the United Arab Emirates, China and Thailand (BIS Innovation Hub, 2023), and a study by the Reserve Bank of Australia (2023) looked at CBDC in payment and settlement services for households and businesses. Some countries are developing their own platforms, while others are working with crypto technology providers such as Ripple and Quant Network. This raises an important concern: fragmentation. If every country launches its own proprietary system, not interoperable with its peers, the benefits of rapid settlement will not be realised. However, it is likely that CBDCs in some form will be well established around the world by 2030.

NON-FUNGIBLE TOKENS (NFTS)

Cryptocurrencies are tokens, but not all tokens are cryptocurrencies. Where tokens are individually unique, they are called non-fungible tokens, or NFTs. These tokens are a record of digital ownership of a unique item, and in some cases have the digital item encoded within them.

Fungibility

Fungibility is an economic property where every unit and sub-unit of an asset can be freely exchanged for another, like pounds and pence, or dollars and cents, or Bitcoin and sats. (A Bitcoin is made up of a hundred million Satoshis, or sats.) A non-fungible token – an NFT – is a unique asset. The neutral description was chosen deliberately because of the vast range of things NFTs could represent.

The first NFT, an animated artwork called Quantum, was created by Kevin McCoy and Anil Dash in 2014 and is an individual token containing a TIF file (Sotheby's 2021). In June 2017, the CryptoPunks collection of 10,000 unique tokens was released, followed by the launch of the first blockchain game, CryptoKitties, in December 2017.

Figure 2.2 A CryptoKitties family (images provided by owner)

Royal Cymric Spock

Calicool | Cymric | Chestnut

Salmon Bloodred Lemonade

CryptoKitties NFTs were the first to be developed under the ERC-721 standard, the blueprint for NFTs. The simple game mechanics allow owners of two CryptoKitty tokens to breed a third that inherits genetic traits from its parents, creating a completely new asset through on-chain automation. CryptoKitties also featured rights of ownership, granting commercial rights to use the specific image relating to an owned token.

NFTs caught the imagination of crypto enthusiasts and fraudsters alike. As the hype grew, there was a proliferation of fake projects, cloned collections and celebrity endorsements luring unwary investors into scams through 'fear of missing out' – the FOMO phenomenon (Financial Conduct Authority, 2022a). The fastest 'rug pull' of the NFT craze, a scam where the perpetrators vanish without trace with the money, was SudoRare, which raised $800,000 in funds and went offline six hours after launch (Sarkar, 2022).

Despite challenging market and regulatory conditions, the basic use case of an NFT, to record ownership of an item and grant rights to the owner, makes them a credible tool for commercial purposes.

DOING THINGS WITH CRYPTO ASSETS

How are crypto assets created and acquired, how do you keep them safe, and what is behind the automation of transactions on a blockchain?

Crypto assets can be acquired in many ways, and once they are acquired, any benefit realised in the form of income or capital gains is taxable in most jurisdictions. Understanding how they can be acquired, whether through payment for goods or services, salaries, gifting, or crypto-specific mechanisms, helps professionals to keep their clients and businesses on the right side of the law. There is more detail on approaches to taxation in Chapter 6.

Minting

Minting is the process of creating an asset on a blockchain, using the same term as for creation of a real-world coin. Assets may be minted by mining and staking (see below) or in game play, for example breeding a new CryptoKitty or earning rewards. However, when we talk of minting as a deliberate action, this usually refers to the creation of NFTs. This could involve an artist uploading their work to a blockchain to offer it for sale, or an investor purchasing a brand new NFT from a collection.

Mining and staking

When a block of transactions is closed on a Proof of Work blockchain like Bitcoin, the miner who is first to solve the block's algorithm receives new coins to be added to the supply. When a block of transactions is closed on a Proof of Stake blockchain, new coins are awarded to a random node to which staking pools have delegated, rather like drawing a raffle. The node then distributes the coins to the owners of the staked tokens. By issuing rewards, users are incentivised to participate in the consensus mechanism and to maintain the security of the chain. We'll look more closely at how these mechanisms work in Chapter 7.

Airdrops

Sending a crypto asset to someone does not require their permission or participation. Deposits made in this way into a user's wallet are known as airdrops. Airdropped assets may be a reward for being part of a crypto community, particularly in gaming. Others may have a more sinister purpose. In a crypto twist on phishing attacks, tokens containing malware can be designed to trick the user into authorising the transfer of their real assets to criminals. However, airdrops can also be used against asset thieves. In November 2022, the High Court ruled that 'proceedings may be served exclusively by non-fungible token (NFT) where no other method of service is available'

(Levy, de Tommaso & Wilde, 2023), with the advantage that the service of legal documents is timestamped on the blockchain.

Keeping assets safe

Crypto assets are kept in wallets. These wallets enable the user to identify themselves on the blockchain and access the assets they own. The wallet may be in the form of a browser extension, an app on a phone, a website, or a physical device that can be connected to a computer when required. Any wallet that is connected to the internet is 'hot'. A wallet that is stored separately, a physical device, is 'cold' until it is connected to the internet. We'll look at the security of crypto assets in more detail in Chapter 3.

SMART CONTRACTS

'A smart contract is a computerized transaction protocol that executes the terms of a contract' (Szabo, 1994). Nick Szabo was a leading figure in the Cypherpunk movement whose members are thought to include the person or persons behind the Bitcoin whitepaper. His smart contract concept was brought to life on the Ethereum blockchain. Every transaction on Ethereum and the blockchains that followed uses a smart contract, although they are not smart, and rarely involve contracts.

The Ethereum whitepaper (2014) describes smart contracts as 'computer programs stored on the blockchain that follow "if this then that" logic'. They enable all the automatic and cryptographically secure processes to take place on the blockchain – mining, minting, staking, transfer of assets, and much more. As with anything that is part of a blockchain, they cannot be changed once they are deployed.

Gas fees

Every transaction on a blockchain incurs a fee, and Ethereum's smart contracts calculate that fee based upon the functions coded into the smart contract, and the level of congestion on the network. Every smart contract is said to consume a certain number of units of gas. The simplest smart contract, the transfer of Ethereum from one wallet to another, uses 21,000 units of gas. This is then multiplied by a variable gas price. The busier the network, the higher the fee, encouraging people to make their transactions when the network is less congested.

If a smart contract is inefficiently coded, it will cost a lot to run. When the network is busy, transaction fees can be extremely high, running into tens or hundreds of dollars depending on the value of ETH at the time. This means that great care must be taken to get the code right before it is used. The history of blockchain is littered with mishaps and hacks resulting from faulty smart contracts. Chapter 7 looks deeper into the technology behind blockchain and recounts some of the cautionary tales.

SAFEGUARDING CRYPTO ASSETS

We know what they are, but how are they protected? The next chapter looks at the security and management of crypto assets, and best practice for individuals and businesses.

Chapter 2 Key takeaways

- Crypto assets (also known as tokens or digital assets) may be fungible or non-fungible.

- Some crypto assets share the properties of money – liquid, exchangeable, and a store of value.

- Cryptocurrencies may be entirely decentralised or issued by corporations and countries.

- Transactions involving crypto assets are automated using smart contracts. Care must be taken when coding a smart contract, as it cannot be changed once deployed.

3 The Keys to a Digital World

Each cryptocurrency, along with any non-fungible crypto assets related to it, runs on its own distributed ledger. This presents unique challenges in securing and using digital assets that may be native to a range of different networks, all with their own proprietary software. It becomes even more complicated if the entity managing assets is not an individual but a company, as there is no way to set up granular access for multiple staff.

Every transaction and every asset on a public blockchain can be viewed on a browser. Figure 3.1 is an extract from the Bitcoin blockchain. It details all the transactions that have involved this randomly selected Bitcoin address, and the current balance of assets held in the owner's wallet.

Figure 3.1 Publicly available information about a Bitcoin address

Bitcoin Address:		
bc1pr52zz02rdzp9va2t7a6y4velkyh3dv3stc6y7r0e0p5gz5l5845qcv8nld		

Bitcoin Balance:	Confirmed Received:	0.00980330 BTC
	Confirmed Spent:	0.00852063 BTC
0.00128267 BTC	Confirmed Unspent:	0.00128267 BTC

Total Transactions: 29

Txn ID:	e7659fcc7135e623614ffd178f55a7890443fe1718de3a4d9347d9bf4fe9ee65	
Timestamp:	12/10/2023, 20:32:00 UTC	
From:	bc1pd86ha79077kvq4ahxsxny8m4qk9kkk75qgnzp3n527f06arrlx4q6kavj0	0.00000940 BTC
To:	bc1pr52zz02rdzp9va2t7a6y4velkyh3dv3stc6y7r0e0p5gz5l5845qcv8nld	Fee: 12.1k Sats

Access to manage rather than simply view the assets is gained through a wallet. This is a user interface that links encrypted, verified credentials to a blockchain. It acts as a login to access on-chain software applications and manage any crypto assets that are associated with those ownership credentials. Every blockchain requires a wallet. For example, the most well-established wallet is MetaMask, serving over 30 million users, but this was designed for the Ethereum blockchain and the ecosystem around it. To manage assets on another chain, you need another wallet.

NOT YOUR KEYS, NOT YOUR CRYPTO

All crypto assets are held in wallets, although there is a distinction between self-custody, in other words, holding the keys to your own wallet, and entrusting a custodian such as a legitimate crypto exchange with your assets. The saying 'not your keys, not your crypto' is a reminder that if you entrust your crypto assets to someone else, you cannot get them back if they end up in the hands of criminals. Scammers will ask for crypto assets to be transferred to their account in order to invest on your behalf for too-good-to-be-true returns, and once money moves out of the banking system there is no cover if something goes wrong.

Blockchains can be viewed on any browser through websites such as blockchain.com/explorer. These browsers can display the details of every transaction on the chain. Crypto tax calculation services use the same data to determine liabilities under relevant tax laws for the user's jurisdiction. The only exceptions are three 'privacy chains' (Monero, Dash and Zcash) that conceal the transaction details, but every other public blockchain is open and transparent.

25

It's vital to protect wallet keys or custodial account login credentials from both compromise and loss. However, being over-cautious leaves no room for error if the medium upon which they are stored is lost.

In this chapter, we will look at the relationship between different blockchains, wallets and exchanges, and outline best practice for crypto asset security.

THE ROLE OF EXCHANGES

You cannot send assets native to the Bitcoin blockchain directly to an address on the Ethereum network, or vice versa. We sometimes refer to individual blockchains as crypto *rails*, and this helps to visualise the role of exchanges in the crypto ecosystem. If you have tickets for the Bitcoin line, you can't leap to an Ethereum train, Mission Impossible style. You have to change at a station where the lines intersect (see Figure 3.2).

Figure 3.2 The crypto rail map

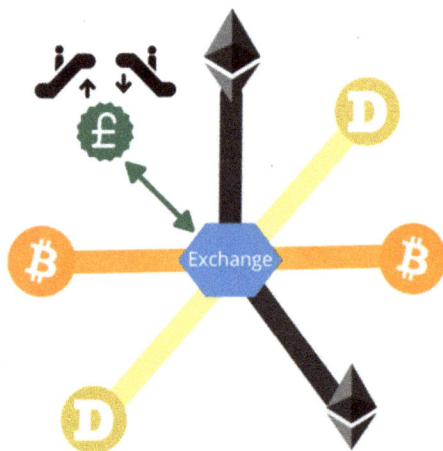

Exchanges are the mainline stations of the crypto ecosystem, allowing users to move value from one rail to another. They will only handle fungible tokens, in other words cryptocurrencies and stablecoins. Exchanges may be centralised, run by a recognisable company and providing the entry and exit points to fiat currencies. Coinbase is a centralised exchange. Alternatively, they may be decentralised, for example Uniswap, using automation (smart contracts) and liquidity provided by users to enable exchange between cryptocurrencies. Decentralised exchanges take advantage of newer technology that enables them to operate across different chains, such as the Inter-Blockchain Communication Protocol that allows direct cross-chain transfer of assets and data.

Using exchanges

Unlike foreign exchange bureaus where we buy fiat (non-crypto) currencies and walk away with our money at the end of the transaction, many centralised crypto exchanges act as custodians; in other words they enable users to keep cryptocurrencies on their account at the exchange.

- Cryptocurrency traders find this useful in times of volatility, ensuring that funds are instantly available for conversion from one asset to another.

- New users are likely to acquire crypto assets by creating an exchange account, transferring fiat currency into it, and buying the cryptocurrency they want. Unless they have a good reason to move their assets onto the relevant blockchains, the funds will stay where they are.

Research in different jurisdictions confirms this. HMRC found that the most frequently mentioned method of acquisition of crypto was through a centralised exchange, by 68% of owners (Fearn, Saunders and Kantar Public, 2022). In Canada, a 2022 Ipsos survey for the Ontario Securities Commission showed that 52% of crypto asset owners 'acquired them through a centralised crypto trading platform, and generally stored them on the exchange or trading platform from where they were purchased' (Fleming et al. 2022).

Figure 3.3 shows a small selection of exchanges that might be used by UK investors. The global landscape is much larger. Website CoinMarketCap lists over 200 spot exchanges that support access for different fiat currencies, and more than 400 active decentralised exchanges, the largest of which are Binance and Uniswap respectively. The majority of centralised exchanges are custodial, in other words they hold funds for their customers. Some also offer self-custody wallets to which their customers can transfer assets.

Figure 3.3 A selection of popular cryptocurrency exchanges

	Centralised	Custodial	Wallet available?	FCA regulated?
Binance	YES	YES	YES	NO
Coinbase	YES	YES	YES	YES
Crypto.com	YES	YES	YES	YES
eToro	YES	YES	NO	YES
Kraken	YES	YES	YES	YES
Solidi	YES	YES	NO	YES
Uniswap	NO - ENTIRELY DECENTRALISED			NO
Uphold	YES	YES	NO	YES
Zengo	NO	NO	YES - WITH RECOVERY	NO

Most of these exchange platforms can be accessed by users anywhere in the world. In the UK, crypto activities are regulated by the Financial Conduct Authority (FCA) but barely a dozen exchange providers have passed their stringent registration process (Franjkovic, 2023). Deposits are not protected through the Financial Services Compensation Scheme (FSCS) as they would be in a bank.

Many exchanges are registered and regulated in other jurisdictions, and we will look at the patchwork of this and wider legislation in Chapter 5.

Exchange security

An exchange is not a bank, but it is easy to be lulled into a false sense of security. The most sophisticated exchanges use the same level of security as a banking app, and the interfaces are well designed and user-friendly. Custodial exchange accounts are secured using biometrics, from fingerprints to comprehensive facial scans, and different multi-factor authentication methods. To register for an account, all registered exchanges must carry out Know Your Customer (KYC) and anti-money laundering (AML) processes, and any account holder who is planning to trade at high volumes can be required to evidence their sources of funds.

> The collapse of unregulated exchange FTX in November 2022, with the loss of $8.7 billion of customer assets, came two months after the FCA issued a warning about its activities (Financial Conduct Authority, 2022b).

An exchange user has several different aspects of security to consider. As with all applications that provide access to valuable assets, it is vital to take due care with personal login credentials, multi-factor authentication methods, and the security of the devices used to access the application. Malware on a computer or smartphone can intercept credentials and mimic authentication pop-ups to enable criminals to take control.

Crypto adds an additional dimension. If the exchange is attacked and funds stolen, can it reimburse its customers? As blockchains are public and transparent, watching the route of stolen funds is straightforward, but recovering them can be harder. And can the exchange itself be trusted? There are many criminals and fraudsters in the industry. Regulation adds a degree of comfort when handing control of your assets to a third party.

Once a business or an individual has dipped their toes into crypto asset ownership through an exchange, the next logical step is to explore the use of crypto wallets. Let's now look at the reasons for moving to a wallet, and how they are secured.

CRYPTO WALLETS AND KEYS

If a custodial account's login details are lost, they can be reset by the exchange company. Wallets, on the other hand, are secured by a pair of keys, public and private encrypted credentials that identify an actor on a blockchain, and they cannot be recovered from a third party. These keys play specific roles and there are different security aspects to consider for each of them. One is always public, while the other must be protected at all costs.

All of the usual warnings about the risks of financial fraud apply equally to the security of crypto assets. As with bank frauds, criminals seek to access wallets directly through the theft of private keys, or use phishing, fake emails and social engineering to make users send funds to the wrong place.

Managing crypto assets comes with its own risks. The process of moving assets from one place to another is not always intuitive or familiar. When a single asset could be worth tens or hundreds of thousands of pounds, and a misstep in the process may result in total loss, moving assets can be a stressful experience.

We suggest some best practice and risk mitigation strategies at the end of this chapter, but first, let's dig into the detail of wallet key pairs: public and private.

Public keys

A public key is the address to which assets can be sent. It's the equivalent of the mailbox at your house, an address visible to everyone. A public key is represented as a long string of letters and numbers, as seen in Figure 3.4. On a browser-based blockchain explorer, you can see the public keys of the parties to each transaction.

Figure 3.4 A transaction on the Ethereum network showing the public keys of both parties

```
Transaction Hash:  0xa7a14eead05da05cde499f362ee6169fe8f18a4a372a0db3072dc8b6a5758322
   Block Height:  19290550
     Timestamp:  6 mins ago (Feb-23-2024 01:20:59 PM +UTC)
        Status:  Success  33 Confirmations
          From:  0xa83114A443dA1CecEFC50368531cACE9F37fCCcb
            To:  0x388C818CA8B9251b393131C08a736A67ccB19297
         Value:  0.19505974229000227 ETH
```

To minimise human error when assets are being moved, it is usual for wallet and exchange apps to have easy one-click copy and paste functions, or to represent a public key with a QR code that can be scanned to populate the send field with the right address. The validity of a public key is also verified automatically with a checksum function as part of the transaction. The chances of a typo generating a valid alternative address are vanishingly small.

In March 2023, investor Brandon Riley paid 77 Eth (around $129,000) for CryptoPunk NFT #685 but made a sending error while working through the complex steps to list it on an investment platform and lost the asset forever. He described the loss as 'the beauty and the curse of self-custody' (Beganski, 2023).

Tools such as the Ethereum Name Service allow users to buy a custom plain-text identifier for their public key – for example, bcs.eth – that acts like a domain name or website address. This helps to ensure that depositors are using the correct public key, and the name appears on the block explorer when a transaction takes place. The identifier is actually an NFT held in the owner's wallet.

Private keys

If the public key is the mailbox, the private key opens the door to the house. Without a private key you cannot access the assets in your wallet. If you are using a custodial exchange account you will only have a public key, because the exchange manages your private key. However, when using your own wallet, you hold the key and have full responsibility for its safety.

When a wallet is set up on a blockchain, part of the process generates a mnemonic phrase of 12 or 24 random words that will enable the holder to retrieve their key and gain access to their assets at any time. Noting down this mnemonic and keeping it safe is *vital*. It is the only way to retrieve access to your wallet and assets in case of emergency.

Try it for yourself

The best way to get first-hand experience of private keys, mnemonic phrases and security is to set up a wallet. This costs nothing and no personal data is shared. Visit https://metamask.io/. Make sure you have reached the right secure website – and follow the instructions.

HOT WALLET OR COLD WALLET?

A cold wallet is one that spends most of its time offline. Popular cold wallets include Ledger Nano and Trezor. These have secure web interfaces that can only be accessed using a specialised USB device. This device, also called a hard wallet, holds the precious private key that enables the owner to use their assets. There are additional security measures built-in, so that simply plugging it into a computer does not provide access. The owner may need to enter a passcode, prompted by the wallet's browser software. If it is corrupted or lost, the original mnemonic phrase provided at setup enables the user to retrieve their private key and set up a new device to access their assets.

As soon as a cold wallet is online, it is no longer cold but hot.

The majority of wallets in use are hot wallets. These may be browser extensions or mobile apps, so they are permanently hosted on a computer or smartphone, rather than sitting in a drawer or a safe. They are accessed using passwords or biometrics and can be regenerated using the mnemonic phrase. MetaMask is a hot wallet. A browser-based hot wallet allows the user to identify themselves to different software applications and activate their assets, walking around Decentraland as a personalised avatar, playing a game on Axie Infinity, or trading NFTs on OpenSea.

Choosing how to manage and secure assets depends on the reasons for acquiring them in the first place.

- Long-term investments are safest in cold storage.
- Interaction with blockchain applications requires the use of online, hot wallets.
- Centralised exchanges provide a route to move value in and out of the crypto ecosystem.

The fundamentals of asset security are common to all of these.

BEST PRACTICE FOR ASSET SECURITY

- Keep the mnemonic phrase for your wallet safe, secure and accessible in case of emergency.

- Avoid using automatic browser or smartphone save features for your wallet or exchange login details. If you must keep these online, use a secure password manager service.

- Use a recognised multi-factor authentication tool such as Authy. Authentication codes sent by SMS or email can be intercepted.

- Check and verify any requests you receive to send money to a cryptocurrency address. The usual phishing scams circulate in the crypto world, but unlike a bank transfer to the wrong address, a crypto transfer cannot be reversed.

- Consider investing in a plain-text wallet address to minimise human error and easily distinguish your brand or nickname from any other public key.

- Ensure that the blockchain from which you are sending is the same as that of the recipient address. You can't send assets across chains.

- Do not attempt to copy a public key by hand. Use copy and paste functions or scan the QR code that many platforms provide.

- Keep your computers and smartphones up to date and use reliable antivirus software to minimise the risk of malware.

- In a corporate setting, put strong safeguards around staff access to a wallet. This is the ultimate Keyman problem. Who has access, who has access in their absence, and can the long-term security of assets in a wallet be guaranteed if there is staff turnover?

What if the worst happens? All is not lost. Every transaction on a blockchain is visible and there are a number of crypto asset forensics and recovery services who are increasingly successful in recovering funds. Industry leader Chainalysis (2023) has helped clients recover $11 billion in stolen crypto. However, the best course of action is to put the foundations of good security in place, safeguarding the keys to a digital world.

USING CRYPTO ASSETS AND BLOCKCHAIN

We know what they are, but how are they used? In the next chapter we will explore live, real-world uses of crypto and blockchain that are already improving business processes, opening up new markets and changing lives.

Chapter 3 Key takeaways

- Not your keys, not your crypto: whoever holds the private key has ultimate control.
- Crypto assets are valuable, and criminals have many strategies to part you from your money.
- Protect your login credentials, private keys and mnemonic phrases from theft or loss.

4   Crypto and Blockchain in the Wild

In the first years of blockchain's existence, the hype surrounding the technology spawned a generation of developers in possession of a groundbreaking technical solution but without a discernible problem to solve. Early experimentation has now given way to practical applications and genuinely innovative ways of working that were not previously accessible.

Both crypto assets and blockchain are being used by individuals and businesses in very different settings to solve problems and improve transparency and record keeping. In this chapter we will look at some of the established and maturing uses of the technology.

OWNERSHIP OF DIGITAL THINGS

Crypto assets allow digital artefacts to be classed as property thanks to the cryptographic proof of legal ownership. This opens a door for the creators of digital things to earn money. The first NFT, Quantum, exists entirely virtually and its artistic and historical value in the traditional art market was demonstrated by its sale at Sotheby's in 2021. Artists don't create exclusively with physical media, and NFTs can provide the missing piece of ownership for digital work (see case study below).

Figure 4.1 Practical uses of crypto and blockchain

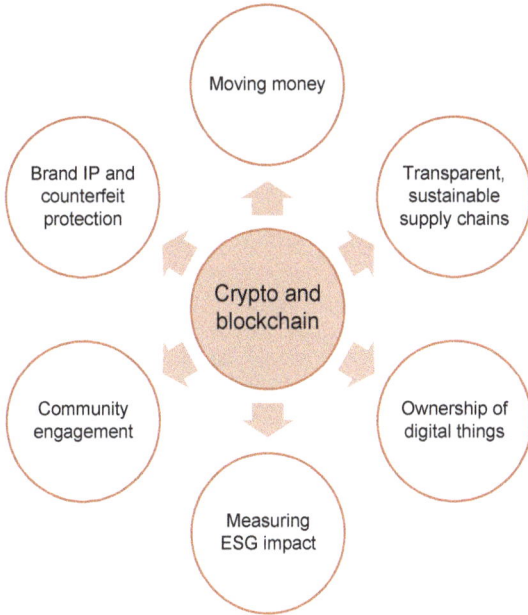

Why does the original matter?

We know the difference between the Mona Lisa on the wall of the Louvre and a poster in the shop. Even if the picture is reproduced with the best materials and framed on our wall at home, we know that it is not the original. The same mindset applies to digital art. The original is provenanced from the hand of the artist through a transparent chain of ownership. A right click to download the JPG file is just a poster.

Digital art, digital ownership

Classically trained fine artist James Atkins was an early adopter of tech, and crypto assets provided the missing piece of digital art ownership. When the first iPads were released, he built a new body of work by drawing and painting directly on-screen. When he was invited to exhibit, there were challenges.

'I printed giclées on massive Epson printers with beautiful, gallery quality paper, very vibrant and then framed,' he explains. 'People were looking at these prints, saying, "Can I buy the original?" There isn't one. It exists digitally, and you're looking at a printout. When I first came across NFTs, I thought, that's it. You don't need to print them because when you do print, something of the original retina display just gets lost. I often used to think about pictures on walls. When was the last time you actually studied a picture on a wall outside of a gallery? You walk past it, they are easily ignored decoration or perhaps just an ownership flex. If Leonardo was around now, he wouldn't be messing around with paint or charcoal on paper. He'd be working at CERN and his art would be embracing technology.'

Figure 4.2 Reproduction of a digital artwork (10x10X #60 by James Atkins, image provided by owner)

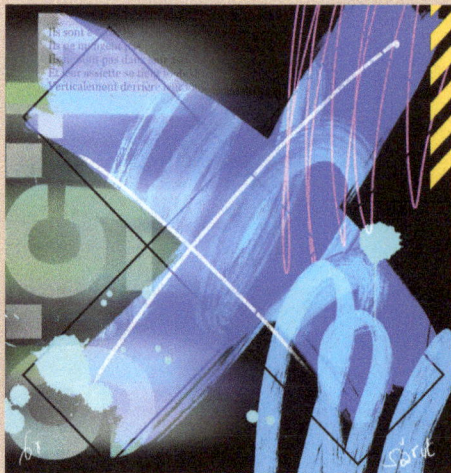

Additional rights may be attached to ownership of an NFT in the real world. If an NFT you own grants VIP access to a concert, for example, presenting the picture in your phone's photo reel at the door does not prove you own it. Showing the NFT in your crypto wallet, with a link to the purchase transaction on the blockchain, is irrefutable proof of ownership and of the rights that go with it.

Blockchain games

Gaming is said to have inspired the creation of Ethereum. Founder Vitalik Buterin, once a keen World of Warcraft player, lost some valuable character features to an arbitrary change by the developers. How could he protect what he viewed as his own property in a centralised system? The idea of actually owning the things into which you have invested time, money and skills is an attractive one. Players already trade assets in traditional games, and blockchain offers immutability of features and protection against trading scams.

Blockchain games accounted for only around 2% of the $350 billion mainstream gaming market in 2023. The crypto crash reduced the value of gaming NFT investments and some projects that had launched with all art and no substance fell by the wayside. However, the industry sees blockchain as a tool to improve business models, and crypto assets as tools for retention, engagement and secure asset trading, and the sector continues to grow.

Beyond art and gaming there is burgeoning interest in the tokenisation of assets and the rights and data attached them, and it is becoming clear that the properties of blockchain can help businesses to solve problems. Let's look at how organisations across other industry sectors are using crypto and blockchain.

COMMUNITY ENGAGEMENT

The Proof of Attendance Protocol (POAP) has provided NFT mementoes – digital badges – for tens of thousands of conferences and events since 2019. More than seven million POAPs have been minted. Some organisations use POAP ownership to reward holders who attended their events in the past.

French football giants Paris Saint-Germain (PSG) use different types of crypto assets as a mechanism for engaging their fan base. The fungible PSG token, of which more than 8 million are in circulation, was issued in 2020. It gives the holder the right to vote on a variety of non-operational, fan-centric decisions such as Goal of the Year, and access to different levels of additional reward depending upon the number of tokens held. For their 2023 tour to Japan, PSG issued premium VIP NFT tickets and a series of commemorative NFTs that included video messages from players. They later offered free NFT collectibles for each of seven matches in their 2023–24 season, with holders entered into matchday draws for club merchandise and experiences (PSG, 2023).

Ticketmaster (2023) offers a similar service to bands, minting NFTs with a right of access to token-gated sales and VIP experiences. They also issue Virtual Commemorative Tickets with some of their packages, NFTs that replace the collectible ticket stubs of old. Sports Illustrated Tickets have launched a blockchain ticketing platform, allowing event organisers to 'engage, reward and stay connected to guests long after the event'.

The advantages for PSG and others are not only continued fan engagement but simplified administration. Unlike formal membership schemes, there is no need to maintain a database of individual fans, reducing data protection and admin headaches. Tokens and their associated benefits can be transferred between fans without any need to update internal records.

More than just a collectible

Successful brand use of crypto assets depends very much on integration in the community engagement strategy and realisation of operational benefits. The market for collectible assets peaked in early 2022 and subsequently crashed dramatically, harmed by an influx of scams and the crash of the crypto and stock markets. A number of high-profile brands announced projects at the peak of the market which have since stalled or did not proceed at all. Between July 2021 and September 2022, Coca-Cola released more than 87,000 branded NFTs, according to the OpenSea marketplace (2023). Bentley (2022) announced a collection but did not launch.

A possible driver of these projects, beyond speculation on the NFT market, may have been the need to establish a verified brand footprint and protect intellectual property (IP) in the virtual world.

BRAND IP PROTECTION

How do you know if that expensive watch is the real thing? This has long been a challenge for luxury goods battling the lucrative counterfeit market, and blockchain and crypto assets offer a solution by recording the individual identity of the genuine articles. There are a number of enterprises addressing the problem, notably the Aura Blockchain Consortium, led by luxury groups LVMH, Mercedes-Benz, OTB, Prada Group and Cartier, and Arianee, serving industries including watches, fashion, wines and spirits, and appliances.

Figure 4.3 Tackling counterfeits with a luxury goods blockchain

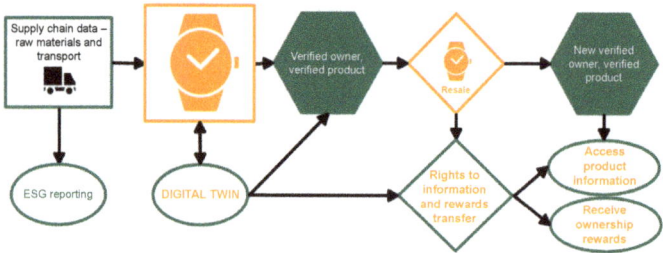

The platforms mint unique digital identities for each product, matched to the physical item by an NFC chip, QR code or other tag embedded in or attached to the product. Customers then claim the digital product passport (DPP) and this activates their identity as owner. DPPs are part of the European Union's plans to enhance transparency on product sustainability and promote eco-friendly products through improved repair and recycling conditions.

Once the DPP is active, the registered owner has access to care and warranty information, with rich content including images and videos added to the record as part of the product lifecycle. Owners can be engaged and rewarded for loyalty through their digital twin ownership in the same way as fan communities.

Brands in virtual worlds

A new challenge for luxury brands is counterfeits in the virtual world. The MetaBirkins NFT collection, minted by artist Mason Rothschild, used the name and style of the iconic Hermès Birkin bag. A New York jury found that the NFTs were commodities, not artworks, and Rothschild had infringed the company's trademark rights (Small, 2023).

Protecting IP in the virtual world is as important as the physical, which is one of the drivers for brands to explore this technology. Virtual world Decentraland's Metaverse Fashion Week (2023) featured the likes of Dolce & Gabbana, Tommy Hilfiger, COACH, Adidas, DKNY, Vogue Singapore, Monnier Paris and others, putting their stamp on a digital presence.

CONSTRUCTION AND CAPITAL PROJECTS

At the opposite end of the industrial scale to digital fashion lies construction, but blockchain and crypto assets are as relevant here as to creators and brands. The Hackitt report (2018) on the Grenfell Fire disaster identified the need for a 'golden thread' of building information. Delivering this lies squarely with blockchain.

Research by Li, Kassem and Watson (2020) highlights the work of Kraken IM whose blockchain-based information management platform allows stakeholders to 'supply, validate and approve engineering data then create an immutable record of that data'. When design change decisions for large capital projects started to be anchored on-chain, Kraken's clients observed greater rigour and care in the decision-making process. Knowing that responsibility for decisions can be evidenced long after the fact influences behaviour.

Materials in construction also present a supply chain challenge as sustainability becomes more important. Defining the carbon load of concrete or steel requires far more complex traceability, and blockchain can already deliver this data, as we will see below.

DIGITAL SUPPLY CHAINS AND SUSTAINABLE TRADE

The EU's plan for a DPP to deliver transparency on product sustainability relies on transparent supply chain systems. Blockchain is the ideal technology for gathering and securing contemporaneous data at all points along the supply chain. In a scoping report for a UK Centre for Digital Trade and Innovation, Short et al. (2022) highlight a need for harmonisation of standards and suggest that the UK must develop a distributed ledger technology innovation programme to stay abreast of other nations.

Fragmented global data standards and regulation present a challenge. Incompatible systems and slow legislation were the downfall of the ambitious TradeLens platform, developed by IBM and Maersk to provide a single, global, interlocking trade solution and mothballed due to a lack of commercial viability (Lopez, 2022). As a case in point, the UK's requirement for paper documentation was only removed in 2023 by the Electronic Trade Documents Act.

Quantifying carbon emissions

The International Finance Reporting Standards (IFRS) Sustainability Disclosure Standards (2023) require carbon emissions data to be reported in filed accounts. Collecting that data from all the way down the supply chain is a challenge that is already being solved. Figure 4.4 shows the prime entries for a three-tier industrial supply chain, recording carbon emissions, compliance documentation and acceptance tests for every stage. The individual data entries and the smart contracts that govern acceptance and emissions calculations can be seen by all the parties to the blockchain.

This simple diagram is based on the far more complex work of Circulor. Founded in 2017, their aim was to deliver traceability and due diligence for raw materials from source to manufacturer. They identified cobalt ore in the electric vehicle (EV) battery supply chain as being the most problematic but essential starting point for their work. Volvo was already seeking to manage the sustainability and ethical sourcing of their new Polestar range, and became one of Circulor's first investors (Campbell, 2020).

As Circulor CEO Doug Johnson-Poensgen says, 'You can't manage what you can't measure.' Prime entry on a blockchain and smart contract automation provides the data needed for measurement and ensures that 'inconvenient truths' cannot be hidden, enabling transparent and pro-active management and reporting.

Figure 4.4 Data transparency in a supply chain

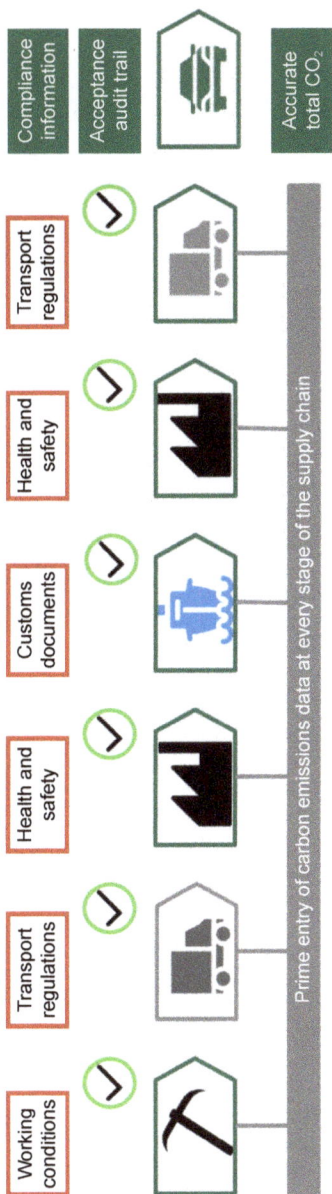

Working conditions

Transport regulations

Health and safety

Customs documents

Health and safety

Transport regulations

Compliance information

Acceptance audit trail

Accurate total CO_2

Prime entry of carbon emissions data at every stage of the supply chain

Tracking transport

How can the sustainability of transport be added into the mix? Reconciling disparate documents and spreadsheets to manage risk data and adjust premiums in arrears was a problem that maritime shipping insurers needed to solve, and blockchain offered a real-time solution. Insurwave, launched in 2018, holds a global asset register and uses smart contracts to manage the insurance transactions when vessels are bought and sold. Sensors on each vessel allow real-time tracking and risk assessments for premium adjustment, for example if the vessel enters a high-risk area such as a piracy or war zone, or based on weather data, port and cargo records, and ship maintenance records (Crawford, 2023).

Combining the transparency of blockchain with AI and big data technologies improves insurance performance, enables more granular analysis including measurement of sustainability, and gives us a clearer picture of the cargos that cross our oceans.

CLOSING THE TRADE FINANCE GAP

It's often the quality of finances, not the quality of product, that keeps a business afloat. The global trade finance gap was estimated at $2.5 trillion in 2022, representing the challenges that small and medium-sized enterprises (SMEs) face in accessing trade finance (Hoffman and Patel, 2023). Supply chain platforms that address the needs of SMEs and smallholders are helping funds trickle down to the people who need them most, and the data they collect is also being used to manage the sustainability of the supply chain.

AgriLedger's blended finance farm-to-table blockchain started life as a project with the World Bank and government of Haiti (Open Access Government, 2019) that aimed to alleviate poverty in the agricultural community. They took simple steps to record the progress of goods from producers to wholesalers to retailers on a transparent ledger. The final acceptance of the negotiated wholesale price was put in the hand of the farmer, and revenue divided between the producer, transporter and negociant by smart contract. This removed price arbitrage, increasing income for farmers, and opened up a wealth of data about the movement of goods.

Di Muto's AgriTrade network started as a way to improve access to trade finance. Farmers were bearing the costs of insurance claims for damaged goods because they could not prove where the damage occurred. Creating a digital twin of a batch of fruit and adding a photograph of its condition at each stage of its journey to market reduced spurious claims. As the audit trail of participation in the supply chain developed, this mitigated risk for finance providers. Producers can access tools such as invoice discounting once acceptance of goods has been confirmed on-chain, improving cash flow and boosting growth.

MOVING MONEY

The vision of using public cryptocurrencies to make everyday payments in the real world is unlikely to become a widespread reality, although there has been enthusiastic adoption in some regions, including countries in South East Asia and Africa where up to a fifth of adults own crypto assets (We Are Social, 2024). In the time that crypto has been evolving, so has financial technology. Whether we are paying with private pounds through our banking apps or by QR code in a Chinese market through WeChat, the process is quick and smooth. As consumers, crypto wallets and volatility present barriers to use. However, the global movement of money increasingly uses crypto technology under the hood.

- In the complex world of repurchase (repo) agreements, a form of short-term borrowing for dealers in government securities, JP Morgan's Onyx platform uses smart contracts and asset tokenisation to settle transfers in real time and reduce risk in liquidity management (JP Morgan, 2023).

- Ripple's foreign exchange management technology was the subject of an early Proof of Concept on improving back-office and foreign exchange processes (Bank of England, 2017) and Ripple now counts Bank of America, PNC Bank, Santander and Standard Chartered among more than a hundred partner banks around the world.

- Tokenised asset transfers tested on the Swift network use existing back-end systems and Chainlink's Cross-Chain Interoperability Protocol (CCIP) (Illgner, 2023).

- Solana's payment infrastructure integrates with e-commerce platform Shopify, providing instant settlement in a dollar pegged stablecoin (USDC) with near-zero transaction fees.

- Nigeria and 19 other African countries have partnered with Coinbase and stablecoin exchange Yellow Card to increase access to the USDC stablecoin and to Bitcoin. These are already gaining traction in day-to-day payments, international payments and hedging against inflation (Chinwe, 2024).

This chapter has highlighted just a handful of applications of crypto and blockchain that are solving business problems. There are many more mature examples and plenty of potential still to be realised. We'll consider some of the emerging applications as part of our look to the future in Chapter 8.

In the next chapter, we will look at the legal and regulatory frameworks that have been established and continue to develop around crypto and blockchain technology.

Chapter 4 Key takeaways

- Crypto and blockchain are valuable elements of the emerging technology stack.

- Start with the problem that needs to be solved before identifying the method to be used.

- New data points and new ways of working are being exposed by blockchain systems.

- Trust and transparency around data collection throughout the supply chain helps companies to fulfil reporting requirements.

5   Staying Legal

The legal structure around crypto assets and blockchain activity is complex and varies markedly from one jurisdiction to another. It's a rapidly evolving area, with new legislation continually in development, and you should check for the latest updates published by government and regulators before taking any action.

This chapter looks at:

- the drivers of crypto regulation
- how and why countries are taking different approaches
- the regulatory structures that emerged in response to the acceleration of crypto and blockchain innovation
- the way that legislation is developed and applied in the United Kingdom, Europe and the United States
- key considerations for individuals and businesses.

The decentralised nature of crypto and blockchain exposes both individuals and smaller businesses to legislative differences between jurisdictions that usually only trouble multinational corporations. The biggest dangers for companies operating in the crypto sector are ensuring that activities that are legal in the country where they are based will not fall foul of the laws where their users live, and that changes in their local laws will not disadvantage them.

The industry is also living with the legacy of the 'Wild West of Crypto'. Some early innovators reasoned that because the technology was new, existing laws did not apply to their activities. Although it's taken time to develop crypto-specific legislation, existing laws have always applied. As law enforcement clamps down, notably in the case of Binance in 2023 (see the case study at the end of the chapter), the rewards for patient and compliant activity are being reaped by careful organisations. The onus is on businesses to ensure they comply with everything, everywhere, all of the time.

Professionals need to know about the legal background to crypto and blockchain because it is increasingly likely that their employers, clients, suppliers or even family members will find themselves using the technology or dealing with crypto assets. This can bring new risks for strategic planning and new business opportunities, internal processes and operations. In Chapter 6 we will also look at implications for insurance, accounting, tax planning and succession.

DIFFERENT COUNTRIES, DIFFERENT LAWS

Every country's approach to crypto asset regulation is influenced by its existing legislative structure and the economic conditions and political imperatives of the jurisdiction. There are growing efforts to achieve global clarity in response to the activities of a borderless industry. The International Organization of Securities Commissions (IOSCO) is consulting on global standards for the regulation of crypto assets (IOSCO, 2023), and the EU is turning its attention to the state of regulation in third countries (Issam, 2023), having issued its first framework for crypto assets across the 27 member states. However, there are still considerable variations in approach across the world.

Figure 5.1 Influences on the development of crypto legislation

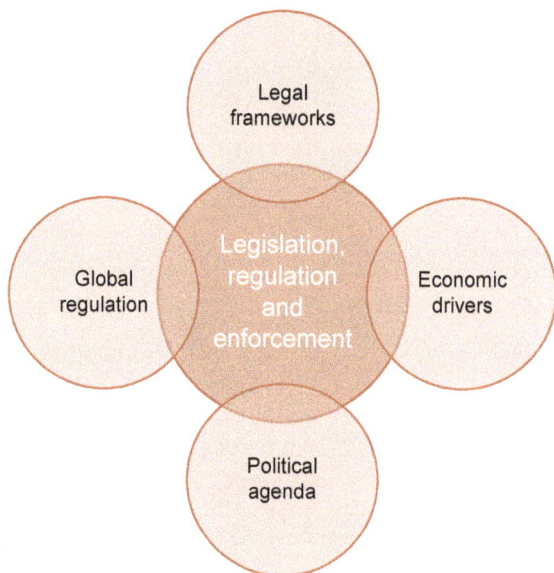

Where legal frameworks and philosophies differ between countries there can be considerable divergence in treatment of the same problem. This can be seen with, for example, privacy laws. In the UK and Europe, the individual's right to privacy is paramount, driven by the European Convention on Human Rights (ECHR) enacted in 1953 in the aftermath of the Second World War, and reinforced by subsequent legislation including the General Data Protection Regulation 2018 (GDPR). Any exceptions to the rule are the subject of case law. This contrasts with the US Constitution's fundamental right to freedom of speech, with exceptions to protect privacy enacted in individual states or at federal level. The resulting divergence came to a head when whistle blower Edward Snowden revealed that data from EU citizens held in US databases was subject to surveillance, rather than being protected to EU standards under an international agreement known as Safe Harbor. Austrian lawyer Max Schrems subsequently sued

Facebook for violations of his personal privacy and the Safe Harbor agreement was declared invalid (Court of Justice of the European Union, 2015).

> Privacy laws are a challenge for blockchain-based systems because data on a blockchain is publicly available and cannot be changed or deleted. Developers of platforms that could be used by anyone living within the jurisdiction of GDPR will be bound by its provisions – and for globally available public blockchains this is likely to happen, regardless of where the company is based.

For crypto regulation, these same US legal structures have resulted in a state-by-state patchwork of legislation and incomplete federal legislation. Crypto-specific bills were due to be debated in Congress in 2022 but were not introduced before the end of the session. This left the federal regulators, the Securities and Exchange Commission (SEC) and the Commodity Futures Trading Commission (CFTC) regulating by enforcement in the absence of guidance. We will look at this in more detail in the section on US legislation later in the chapter.

Economic drivers

Attracting high value crypto businesses to a location can make economic sense. Early regulatory frameworks established in New York, Zug, Gibraltar, Malta and Wyoming paid dividends as exchanges moved in – Kraken to Wyoming and Binance to Malta. They also welcomed new enterprises rich from selling cryptocurrency tokens to finance their project development.

Kazakhstan took a more direct approach in 2017, attracting Bitcoin miners with 'cheap energy and loose regulation'. When relations turned sour five years later, this 'parasitic industry' was banned, and the government is now taking steps to 'turn the country into a global crypto finance hub... to kick-start its finance and tech sectors' (Guest, 2023).

Political agenda

Establishing a global crypto hub is a familiar political rhetoric. Plans are in place to make Britain a 'global hub for crypto asset technology and investment' (HM Treasury, 2022). CoinDesk's 2023 global crypto hub rankings have Zug in first place followed by Singapore, London, Seoul, Dubai and Abu Dhabi (Mersetzky, 2023). But how well does this ambition sit with regulators? The FCA has been fiercely protective of consumers and investors, and its former chair, Charles Randell, believes that the government has 'failed to quantify the consumer harms that could result from holding crypto out as a regulated investment' (O'Dwyer, Asgari and Pickard, 2023). This friction provides checks and balances but can be a source of frustration on both sides.

Financial Action Task Force

The Financial Action Task Force (FATF) is the global money laundering and terrorist financing watchdog. It sets international standards that aim to prevent illegal activities and the harm they cause to society. Its standards on Virtual Assets and Virtual Asset Service Providers are gradually being rolled out across member countries (FATF, 2023), rare common regulatory ground across multiple jurisdictions.

One standard invokes Travel Rules, requiring transparency on crypto asset transfer transactions. They are part of the toolkit of AML and counter-terrorism financing (CTF), aimed at preventing criminals from passing cryptocurrencies through exchange accounts. A large part of the criminal case brought against Binance (US Department of Justice, 2023) involved violations of AML and CTF laws.

In practice, the Travel Rules mean that exchanges require the name of the recipient for any withdrawals and the name of the sender for any deposits, and can freeze accounts for manual reviews. A growing group of Virtual Asset Service Providers (VASPs) have collaborated to implement a compliance standard, TRUST, bringing the global industry into a common system.

EARLY CRYPTO LAWMAKING

By the time the Mt. Gox exchange collapsed in 2014 (see Chapter 1), legislators and regulators were sitting up and taking notice. In 2015 in the United States, the New York State Department of Financial Services issued a license for virtual currency activities (NYDFS, 2023), becoming the first jurisdiction to regulate the industry. Several companies left the state seeking less burdensome environments, but others including the Coinbase exchange remained (del Castillo, 2015).

Most individual US states rely on existing money transmission licences for crypto businesses. Notable exceptions are New York, whose 2015 BitLicense marked the start of crypto-specific regulation in the US; Rhode Island and Washington, who require specific disclosures and protections (Bloomberg Law, 2022); and Wyoming, whose 2019 blockchain and digital asset laws established a welcoming framework for crypto businesses (Long, 2019).

The Ethereum blockchain, launched in 2015, was the first to include an application layer that allowed innovators to build on the platform. This resulted in an explosion of blockchain projects. In response, several countries chose to boost their economies by providing regulatory frameworks for blockchain activity. Businesses moved in, reassured by the certainty that the legislation provided.

The Swiss canton of Zug, home of the Crypto Valley Association, started accepting Bitcoin payments for municipal taxes as early as 2016, and other parts of Switzerland have followed this example. In 2017, Gibraltar became the first jurisdiction to provide a clear and comprehensive regulatory framework for blockchain and cryptocurrency businesses, enacting its Financial Services (Distributed Ledger Technology Providers) Regulations (Gibraltar Laws, 2017). Malta's 2018

Innovative Technology Arrangements and Services Act and Virtual Financial Assets Act took a flexible, technology-first approach to allow adaptations to guidance as the technology evolved (Wolfson, 2018). All three of these jurisdictions now host maturing blockchain and crypto companies and a lively technology ecosystem.

Figure 5.2 Early regulatory frameworks in Europe

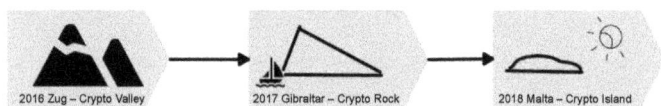

2016 Zug – Crypto Valley   2017 Gibraltar – Crypto Rock   2018 Malta – Crypto Island

Other countries were also developing their own frameworks during this time. A paper in the Law Library of Congress (2018) outlines progress in Argentina, Australia, Belarus, Brazil, Canada, China, France, Iran, Israel, Japan, Jersey and Mexico, as well as Gibraltar and Switzerland. Singapore has also embraced blockchain technology, supporting a number of projects through the Monetary Authority of Singapore, but is cautious about crypto assets.

Global regulation is advancing, and we will now focus on three key jurisdictions – the United Kingdom, Europe and the United States.

UNITED KINGDOM

Crypto asset policies in the UK mark key steps in the country's efforts to provide certainty for businesses and protection from criminality. The progress of legislation is regularly updated on government websites, and consultation papers are issued by the Law Commission and the FCA to gather industry expertise in forming and refining laws. The FCA, the Payment Services Regulator (PSR) and the Bank of England are responsible for regulating and enforcing the laws that are passed.

Figure 5.3 The legislative and regulatory cycle of the United Kingdom

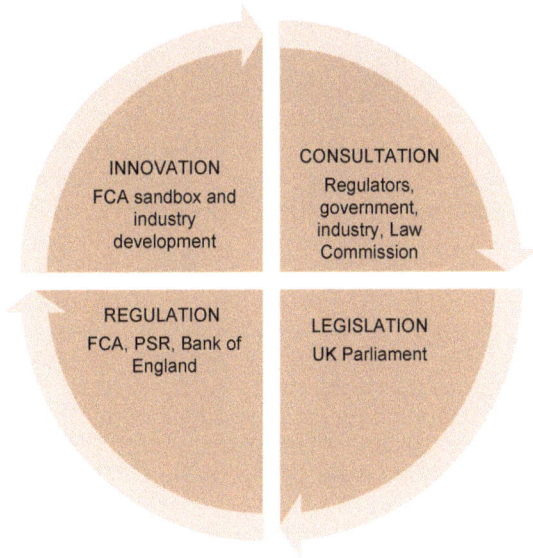

The FCA has an innovation programme, the Regulatory Sandbox, that includes blockchain and crypto activities. It is designed to support technology businesses that are looking to deliver innovation in the UK financial services market to UK consumers or firms (FCA Innovation Hub, 2023). This initiative was first established in 2012 and has helped to cement the UK's position as a leader in financial technology.

In their 2023 paper on crypto asset consumer research, the FCA states that no regulatory regime can offer market integrity or consumer protection for crypto asset activities to the same degree as for traditional financial instruments. This stems from the cross border, fragmented nature of crypto, the pseudonymity of wallets, and the lack of corporate issuers of decentralised financial instruments (Aju and Burrell, 2023). This is a challenge not just for the UK but for all centralised regulators faced with activities that are taking place across the world on decentralised platforms.

Regulations governing crypto asset activities

UK crypto asset businesses are required to register with the FCA and to comply with the Money Laundering, Terrorist Financing and Transfer of Funds (Information on the Payer) Regulations 2017 (the MLRs). This applies to crypto asset exchange and ATM providers, peer to peer providers, issuers of new crypto assets, and custodian wallet providers (HMRC, 2024b).

Between the first UK registration of a crypto business in 2020 and the approval of PayPal in late 2023, only 43 crypto companies had achieved MLR compliance despite several hundred applications being submitted. The slow and stringent process has seen companies leave the UK to seek registration elsewhere and serve their customers from offshore (Noonan, Oliver and Venkataramakrishnan, 2022).

Legislation is constantly being rolled out and regulators are acting on it. The UK Financial Services and Markets Act 2023 (FSMA) brought crypto assets including NFTs into the scope of the existing Regulated Activities and Financial Promotions regimes. In October 2023, as the first part of implementing the legislation, financial promotions regulations came into force for crypto businesses (FCA, 2023). These restrict advertising to FCA-registered businesses and require a cooling-off period for new investors, itself a tricky thing to achieve when crypto transactions are finalised almost instantly. On the first day, the FCA issued 146 warnings of promotions by unregistered companies (O'Connor, 2023), highlighting many scams and fraudulent schemes.

In the same period, the FCA categorised Bitcoin and other cryptocurrencies as 'restricted mass market investments' and from January 2024 required crypto exchanges to conduct client appropriateness testing. This asks users to self-certify as high net worth individuals or to declare their income in order to continue trading and investment activities.

The FATF Travel Rule came into force for users of crypto exchanges in the UK in December 2023.

Recent Economic Crime and Corporate Transparency legislation updates rules on the seizure of assets to include all types of crypto, or intangible, assets. The Law Commission's recommendations on legal principles and frameworks for digital assets are also gradually making their way into UK legislation.

EUROPE

The European Union believes that crypto activities are sufficiently different from other financial activities as to require their own regulatory framework. They started early in developing comprehensive single market legislation with the aim of enabling crypto and blockchain innovation throughout the bloc, while building in a clear appreciation of risk. The Markets in Crypto-Assets Regulation 2023 (MiCA) went through several years of rigorous consultation with the crypto asset industry and all 27 countries, and will be the subject of continuous review as the landscape evolves. For example, there is no specific mention of NFTs in the existing legislation thanks to the lag between consultation and enactment, and these will be addressed in the next round of amendments.

MiCA lays out specific rules on the transparency, disclosure, authorisation and supervision of transactions. Crypto asset services, which include any professional entity or person providing exchange services or dealing advice, are subject to consumer protection, transparency and governance standards, and are required to protect against cyber-attacks, theft or malfunction. Anyone offering services under MiCA must have a registered office in a member state and be authorised in that state. Third-country firms can be used by European citizens, but these firms cannot solicit clients or promote and advertise their services, and if they try to do this they need to go through the process of authorisation or face sanctions.

MiCA provides a strong foundation for comprehensive and joined-up legislation around crypto activities. However, aspects of crypto and blockchain technology conflict with other EU legislation. For example, the need to protect personal data and exercise a right to be forgotten under GDPR means developers must avoid putting identifiable information on-chain, even if encrypted. The Data Act (European Commission, 2024), which will apply from September 2025, has also sparked industry concern over its provisions for smart contracts, the automation tools of blockchain. These include sensible measures – robustness and access control, auditability and data archiving – but also safe termination and interruption, which will be hard to achieve and impossible to retrofit.

UNITED STATES

Europe's enabling single market approach contrasts with the far more fragmented and rigid legislation of the United States. Where Europe is taking a top-down view of legislation that is then adopted by its 27 member states, there is a disconnect in the US between 50 sets of state-level legislation (very few of which are adapted to crypto and blockchain activities), and federal legislation that is intended to provide guidance to regulators, the SEC and the CFTC.

The SEC and CFTC opinions on crypto assets differ. The CFTC has determined that virtual currencies are commodities under the Commodity Exchange Act (CEA). The SEC, on the other hand, treats every crypto asset other than Bitcoin as a security, and has aggressively pursued crypto asset issuers and exchanges for not registering their activities, while a method of registration remains unclear. This approach has been criticised as 'regulation by enforcement' by the industry in lieu of a clear rule book.

In addition to the federal regulators, the Department of Justice has a National Cryptocurrency Enforcement Team. This was established to address 'the criminal misuse of cryptocurrencies and digital assets... by virtual currency exchanges, mixing and tumbling services, infrastructure providers, and other entities'.

In the 2023 prosecution of Binance Holdings Ltd (see case study), the Department of Justice and CFTC emphasised that all companies carrying out crypto activities must follow the law. They called on Congress to bring legislation forward to fill gaps in the existing guidance, raising hopes that the divergence between the CFTC and SEC interpretation of existing laws can be resolved and bring clarity to crypto businesses.

In January 2024, the SEC approved the sale of Bitcoin Exchange-Traded Funds in mainstream investment markets, although they made it clear in their decision that this was not an endorsement of Bitcoin itself, and their actions against exchanges and crypto companies continue.

The Binance story

The Binance exchange was established in China in 2017 and grew rapidly, gaining six million customers in nine months. Founder Changpeng Zhao (CZ) relocated the business when cryptocurrency trading was banned in China. The first port of call was Japan, where regulators issued a warning after Binance failed to register its activities (Zhao, 2018). CZ then moved Binance's operations to Malta where new crypto-specific legislation had been enacted, but withdrew its application for a licence just a year later in 2019.

Over the next few years, as Binance expanded to over 120 million users worldwide, the organisation became increasingly opaque, refusing to disclose where its headquarters were located, and its response to regulatory requirements became fragmented. In 2021, the FCA warned that Binance was 'not capable of being supervised properly', refusing registration to its UK arm, Binance Markets Ltd, despite the UK leadership's best efforts at meeting regulatory conditions and participating in legislative consultations.

In the United States, local arm Binance US gained its federal Money Services Business registration and its exchange subsidiary held state-level money transmission licences. However, legal action was brought against the entire global corporation for deliberately avoiding regulations and laws by not registering itself as a money service, or implementing anti-money laundering compliance. This action was led by the Department of the Treasury's Financial Crimes Enforcement Network (FinCEN), the Office of Foreign Assets Control (OFAC) and the CFTC – but not the SEC, who continue to pursue separate action for unregistered securities trading.

The Treasury and CFTC action concluded in November 2023 with a guilty plea from Binance and CZ himself. A fine of $4.3 billion was levied for 'consistent and egregious' violations of law, enabling the funding of criminals, sanctioned parties and terrorist organisations, and putting profits over the interests of the American people. The company continues to operate in the US under monitoring organised by FinCEN and with strict additional compliance requirements in place for five years.

Separate action by the SEC against Binance and other exchanges continues.

In the next chapter we will look at the legislation that affects people and organisations – taxation, accounting, insurance legacy planning, asset protection and blockchain-specific legal risks.

Chapter 5 Key takeaways

- Crypto legislation, regulation and enforcement are approached in different ways by individual states and countries, resulting in a fragmented and inconsistent approach.

- It is difficult for centralised regulators to deal with a decentralised structure.

- Always check the regulations that apply to your business and to your customers elsewhere in the world.

6　Death and Taxes

'In this world, nothing is certain except death and taxes.' Although Benjamin Franklin wrote this in the late eighteenth century, the same applies to the new world of crypto.

When dealing with professional clients, enterprises or family members, simply asking if they have any other assets or activities to discuss with their accountant or lawyer may not reveal the risks that exist, especially if someone is wrongly convinced, for example, that crypto isn't taxable and they don't need to mention it.

Asking specific questions about crypto assets and related activities can change the way that you approach taxation, legacy and succession planning, custodianship, insurance, and other risks of decentralised activity. Failing to ask the right questions might expose advisors to claims of negligence if something goes wrong.

KEY RISKS AND QUESTIONS TO ASK

1. Has your client, employer or family member ever owned a crypto asset? Where did they get it and what did they do with it?

2. Are tax returns up to date including income, gains and losses from crypto activity?

3. How are the private keys and exchange logins protected? Are they insured to the value of the assets to which they give access, and by whom?

4. How are crypto assets reflected in financial statements?

5. What if the worst happened? Could executors access crypto holdings, and is it clear who the beneficiaries are?

6. If a business is working with crypto or blockchain in any form, does their insurance cover these activities?

7. Do any tokens give the owner decision-making power in a Distributed Autonomous Organisation (DAO)?

Let's look at the underlying issues in more detail.

Figure 6.1 Crypto risks for businesses and individuals

TAXATION

When early rises in cryptocurrency values resulted in windfalls for investors, many assumed that these gains were tax free because crypto was such a new concept. However, taxes on income and capital gains apply to any asset, across every tax jurisdiction. Tax authorities can read a public ledger and most have information-sharing agreements with exchanges. They may well know what you're doing before you even consider filing your taxes.

Individuals and businesses are taxed on their crypto activity in the jurisdiction in which they are tax resident, regardless of where in the world the taxable event occurred. *Treatments depend upon your jurisdiction and you are advised to take local advice.*

Help is at hand for tax returns. Platforms such as Koinly use APIs from exchanges and blockchains to construct a double-entry ledger of your crypto activity, reducing the need for manual calculations. They also act as a useful dashboard of your entire portfolio. Tax platforms determine the treatment of each transaction according to your specified jurisdiction and can generate appropriate reports to be submitted with your return. Transactions involving decentralised finance (DeFi) activities and some NFTs may need manual adjustments.

The first HMRC tax guidance for crypto assets was issued in 2014 and is continually being updated through industry consultation as crypto activities and the assets themselves evolve. The comprehensive Cryptoassets Manual (HMRC, 2024a) contains clear and detailed guidance for individuals, businesses and advisors.

The interplay of income tax and capital gains tax (CGT) is complex. The manner of acquisition of a crypto asset and the relative values of different crypto assets and fiat currency at the time of related transactions must be taken into account, as demonstrated in Figure 6.2.

Figure 6.2 Taxes on movement of crypto assets

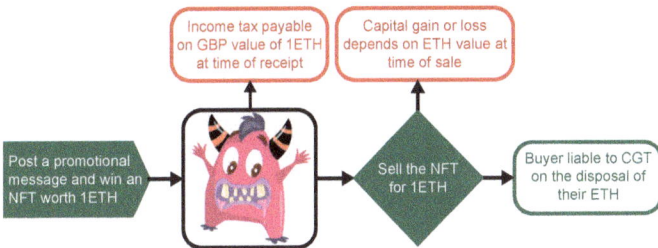

- Income tax applies to mining and staking, and to receipt of crypto assets in return for a service. This service could be as simple as posting marketing material on social media at the request of a crypto project.

- Tokens are a chargeable asset if they are capable of being owned and have a value that can be realised.

- A disposal occurs if a token is exchanged for a different type of token. This means that buying an NFT using ETH results in a disposal of ETH and the acquisition of the NFT, and capital gains tax applies to the transaction.

- Published capital gains tax guidance covers everything from S104 pools to forks in a blockchain and crystallising capital losses if private keys are lost.

Decentralised finance

There are complexities around lending and staking within DeFi – not to be confused with staking tokens as part of a Proof of Stake consensus mechanism (see Chapter 7). Participation in yield farming or liquidity pools involves transfers of capital, in other words disposal and subsequent re-acquisition of assets, and earnings are treated as income.

Liquidity pools are particularly tricky. These are made up of pairs of tokens and the balance of the pairs will change over time as relative asset values fluctuate. This means that when assets are withdrawn from a liquidity pool, they may be in a different proportion to the original transfer. HMRC offers detailed guidance on how gains, losses and allowable costs can be calculated.

LEGACY PLANNING

As we saw in Chapter 3, it's vitally important to keep the keys to your crypto assets out of the hands of criminals. Unfortunately, security can be taken to an extreme, and there are no easy answers on the best way to manage your keys should the worst happen. The information below discusses individual legacy, but the same tools for protecting wallet keys and valuable assets offer solutions for businesses who need to retain ownership while allowing different team members to interact with their assets.

Any of these options might be viable, but there are challenges to consider with them all.

Volatility and insurance

Does your advisor have adequate insurance to hold your keys? What if your friend or your family members lose or use the envelope you gave them? Holding the keys to 10,000 Bitcoin when that was just enough to buy two pizzas was a negligible risk, but safeguarding the same number of coins today is a very different matter, running into hundreds of millions of pounds.

Figure 6.3 Options for safeguarding crypto keys

Ownership of assets

What are the legal implications of using a specialised crypto key storage service? It all comes down to definitions of ownership of assets. The legal owner holds the title to assets, like the title deeds of a house. The equitable, or beneficial, owner can benefit from the asset, which means they can live in the house. In most cases, we are both the legal and equitable owners of our assets. If assets are placed into trust, the ownership splits. Trustees become the legal owners but are not the beneficiaries. Assets may be tangible or intangible, although the Law Commission has recommended that future digital asset legislation defines a new third category of 'thing' to handle the special features of crypto assets (Cross, 2023), and we will see how and if this changes the landscape in years to come.

London-based AssetPass allows users to upload wallet keys and NFTs and other valuable digital assets, and has a secure 'Trustee Release Control Process' in place for access by the original owner or by their nominated beneficiaries. This raises a few questions about who is the legal owner of the assets (has a trust been formed?) and there could be a conflict between who has been nominated to access the assets, and who is named as a beneficiary in an official will.

Social recovery wallets are also becoming more popular. These allow the owner to nominate guardians, who could be friends, family, professional advisors or team members in a business. These guardians can vote to restore access to the wallet if the keys are lost. It's a useful approach but could backfire if the nominated guardians override a living asset owner to take control. There is also the same question of whether the nominated guardians and the beneficiaries named in a will are the same people, and it is vital that intentions are made clear before any of these processes are put in place.

> Don't leave this to chance. The deathbed sharing of a five-digit code was all that executors had to go on in a recent case. Luckily, the code was traced to a hard wallet, but there could have been a very different outcome.

Paper wills

In the UK, the Wills Act 1837 still applies. This act pre-dates the availability of electric power by several decades, let alone computers, and every will has to be signed, in ink, with witnesses. In the United States, the Uniform Electronic Wills Act 2019 represents some progress towards the use of digital media, but as with all US legislation it has to be adopted by each state and the process is slow. The UK Law Commission is consulting on digital wills, but there are protections afforded by witnessed paper wills that cannot be replicated digitally. Blockchain may address some (but by no means all) of the problems, for example verifying the authenticity of a document.

Legacy planning is complex, but not as difficult as chasing down assets in a blind treasure hunt after the fact. Investing time and money in proper planning and will writing can avoid ambiguity, arguments and much greater costs in the future.

This applies equally to businesses who can access the same expertise to establish effective governance and navigate the complexities of safeguarding assets before anything untoward occurs.

INSURANCE

'We will not pay for claims or losses arising from purchase, use or development of blockchain, non-fiat currencies, smart contracts or non-fungible tokens.'

This is becoming a common exclusion in business insurance as the industry tries to model the risks of volatile asset values, criminal activity, immature software applications and immutable smart contracts. There are a number of specialist insurers who are experienced in handling more nuanced blockchain and crypto risk, but many others will refuse cover if an enterprise is moving into this sector.

It is important to check the following:

- Will your insurance cover you for the full value of your assets if the private keys are lost or stolen?

- Will your insurance cover the asset value if you agree to take custody of your client's private keys for safekeeping or legacy planning purposes?

- Will your insurance cover losses arising from the development of blockchains and smart contracts, for instance if a smart contract you build has a flaw?

Smart contract errors may be the greatest risk for developers. In 2021 alone, $680 million of digital assets was hacked or stolen due to vulnerabilities in smart contracts (Sharma et al., 2022). Smart contracts that are compromised pose a significant risk. If a user has authorised a smart contract to interact with their wallet, criminals could use this to access the assets held there. This can be avoided by revoking authorisations (Ethereum, 2023).

Figure 6.4 Losses from smart contract flaws

BNB	Poly Network	Pickle Finance
Attackers minted 2 million BNB tokens for free, but the attack was stopped and all but $110 million of stolen funds frozen or recovered.	A white hat hacker was able to reallocate $600 million funds to their own wallet, which they returned. A bug bounty program was set up.	A fake savings jar was created on this DeFi app and $19.7 million deposits diverted and stolen.

ACCOUNTING FOR CRYPTO ASSETS

Crypto assets cause headaches for accountants. The application of International Accounting Standards (IAS) in different countries is changing over time as the nature of the assets becomes clearer. The prevailing treatments in your jurisdiction may differ from the basic principles below.

- Crypto assets are intangible, so IAS 38 Intangible Assets was the obvious starting point for standard setters. However, this requires crypto assets to be measured at cost and amortised, which does not reflect their volatility or real nature. In the US, the Financial Accounting Standards Board (FASB) added a new rule stating that from December 2024 US businesses must use fair-value accounting for fungible crypto assets (FASB, 2024).

- Crypto assets may also be inventory, held for sale in the normal course of business. In this case, they are covered by IAS 2 Inventories.

As cryptocurrencies are not considered to be money, IAS 21 The Effects of Changes in Foreign Exchange Rates does not apply. IFRS 9, Financial Instruments, may apply to any crypto asset-based securities, such as Exchange-Traded Funds (ETFs).

DISTRIBUTED AUTONOMOUS ORGANISATIONS

The idea of Distributed Autonomous Organisations (DAOs) started as a shared investment concept in 2016, The DAO, that was famously hacked at launch.

The DAO

The original DAO was an automated shared investment concept, The DAO, that existed very briefly in 2016. Smart contracts would identify the best of the best applications for investment and maximise the return for participants. It was wildly successful. Investors added around $150 million to the pot – around 14% of all the Ethereum in circulation at the time. Unfortunately, a few days before The DAO went live, the founders spotted a potential flaw in the smart contract. They were not the only ones. On launch day, 17 June 2016, they could only watch as an attacker drained the funds.

This was so early in the development of Ethereum that for the first and only time the blockchain was forked, three days after the hack, at block 1,920,000. A new smart contract then sucked all the original DAO investments into a special account (Detrio, 2017) and investors were able to recover their money. The fork created a new chain, Ethereum Classic. Comparing the fork blocks on the two chains reveals that their block hash is different – a clear indication that the chains have diverged (see Chapter 7).

Since then, the idea has evolved and embraces everything from decentralised finance and software development to global social impact collaborations and community engagement. A DAO will usually be initiated by a single organisation or several in collaboration and gradually move towards decentralisation as the governance model matures. There is a lot of interest in this structure as it aligns with the global distributed nature of blockchain. In 2023, DAO treasuries, including decentralised exchange Uniswap's DAO, reportedly held more than $25 billion of assets (Young, 2023).

73

The first step to mitigating risk is to understand the nature of an individual or company's involvement. Is participation in a DAO through token ownership generating any taxable income? Is it the equivalent of holding shares (which opens a whole new can of securities law worms)? Is there a legal risk of inadvertent partnership and personal liability for the actions of the DAO?

For the creators of a DAO, voting by a community of token holders to trigger an automated action is fraught with governance and participation risks. What if a coalition of malicious actors has enough tokens to sway the vote and change the direction of travel of the organisation? Developing a viable governance model is essential and this has to reflect the underlying structure, for example, deferring the final decision from an advisory vote to a smaller expert council, or restricting votes to non-operational matters as a simple community engagement exercise. DAOs show promise, but they are not yet fully formed, and risks must be taken into account.

A DEEPER DIVE

We've looked at the nature of crypto assets, the ways that they are used and protected, the applications in business, and the legal, regulatory and administrative structures and risks that surround them. But what is the infrastructure of crypto and blockchain? In the next chapter, we go deeper into the technology to expand your understanding of what it is, and how it is best used to solve business problems.

Chapter 6 Key takeaways

- There are many different risks for businesses and individuals to manage.

- A duty of care may exist for professional advisors and employers.

- It is important to seek professional advice on securing assets for business use or legacy planning.

7 Crypto Under the Hood

Every crypto asset runs on a blockchain, but blockchains themselves have an important place in the modern technology stack, as we saw from some of the applications in Chapter 4. Now let's examine the structure and properties of blockchains and show how they achieve the properties of trust, transparency and decentralisation. We'll also outline the different types of platforms that are available and see when blockchain might be appropriate, or not, as a solution to business problems.

HASHED DATA

Blockchain security relies upon cryptographic techniques, particularly the ability to produce unique hashes to summarise large amounts of data. Hashing is the process of assigning a numeric or alphanumeric string to a piece of data. The same technology lies behind end-to-end encrypted messaging systems, although there are many different encryption methods in use in blockchain applications to maximise security of the chains and the assets they hold.

You can experiment with hashing using free online tools to generate SHA-256 (256-bit encryption) hashes for words and phrases, or even entire books, invoices, certificates and transaction records. Changing one character will change the hash, as in Figure 7.1. This allows us to trust matching hashes, verifying that the underlying data is unchanged if the hash is the same.

Figure 7.1 Hashing a sentence then changing one character

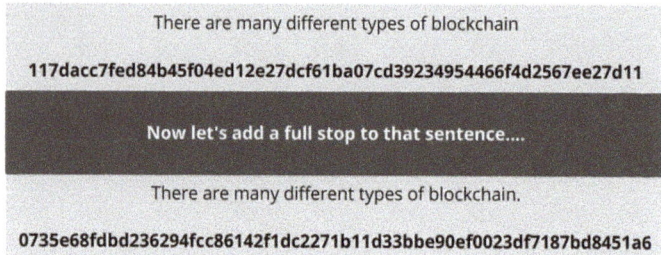

There are many different types of blockchain

117dacc7fed84b45f04ed12e27dcf61ba07cd39234954466f4d2567ee27d11

Now let's add a full stop to that sentence....

There are many different types of blockchain.

0735e68fdbd236294fcc86142f1dc2271b11d33bbe90ef0023df7187bd8451a6

Quantum computing may threaten current encryption methods as early as 2030, and work has been underway for more than a decade to develop quantum-resistant cryptographic algorithms. This means that data we encrypt now could be read in the future – so be careful about exactly what is recorded on-chain.

A CHAIN OF BLOCKS

A blockchain is a distributed ledger where transactions are batched into blocks and each block is connected to the previous and the next block in the chain. Figure 7.2 shows the basic structure of three block headers in an imagined chain.

- The block height shows its position in the chain.

- Each block is timestamped to the second, confirming the time and date of prime entry into the chain for any transaction in that block. Each transaction also has its own timestamp marking the point at which it entered the network, to avoid duplication.

Figure 7.2 A chain of blocks

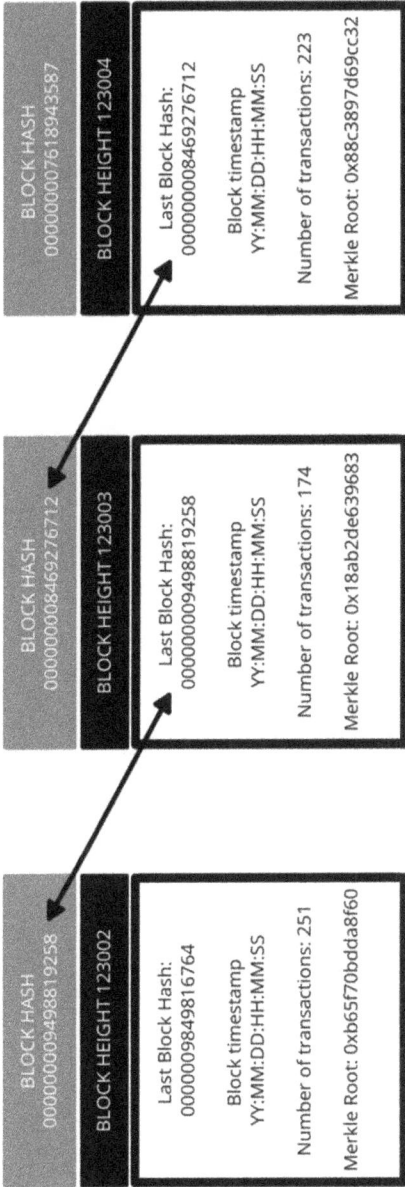

BLOCK HASH
0000000094988 19258

BLOCK HEIGHT 123002

Last Block Hash:
0000000984816764

Block timestamp
YY:MM:DD:HH:MM:SS

Number of transactions: 251

Merkle Root: 0xb65f70bdda8f60

BLOCK HASH
0000000084692 76712

BLOCK HEIGHT 123003

Last Block Hash:
0000000094988 19258

Block timestamp
YY:MM:DD:HH:MM:SS

Number of transactions: 174

Merkle Root: 0x18ab2de639683

BLOCK HASH
0000000076189 43587

BLOCK HEIGHT 123004

Last Block Hash:
0000000084692 76712

Block timestamp
YY:MM:DD:HH:MM:SS

Number of transactions: 223

Merkle Root: 0x88c3897d69cc32

- A block can contain hundreds or thousands of transactions.

- The Merkle root is the hash of all the hashes of all the transactions that are part of the block. This makes the block header as small as possible and gives us a single hash reference to verify that none of the underlying transactions have been tampered with.

- The block hash represents all the contents of the header – not just the timestamp and transactions but also the hash of the previous block. If there is any attempt to change a transaction, this would change the block hashes of every subsequent block all along the chain, and the system will not allow this to happen. Data on a blockchain is therefore unchangeable, or immutable.

Immutable means that something is unchangeable. **Immutability** is the basis of trust in blockchain records, as any change to transactions that have already been added to the chain will not be accepted by the **consensus mechanisms** that secure the system.

VISUALISING THE DISTRIBUTED BLOCKCHAIN

Anyone who chooses can hold a blockchain on their computer and become one of the nodes of the distributed ledger. The largest blockchain, that of Bitcoin, was estimated to use 500GB of disk space in 2023 and is growing by approximately 1MB (the size of a block) every ten minutes. Nodes receive transactions at random from users, the blockchain's software runs automatic validation checks, then accepted transactions are added to the next proposed block. In the event that a transaction is inadvertently duplicated, for example an impatient user clicking to submit more than once, only the first to be timestamped will be added to the chain, as with Transaction A in Figure 7.3.

Figure 7.3 Visualising a distributed ledger

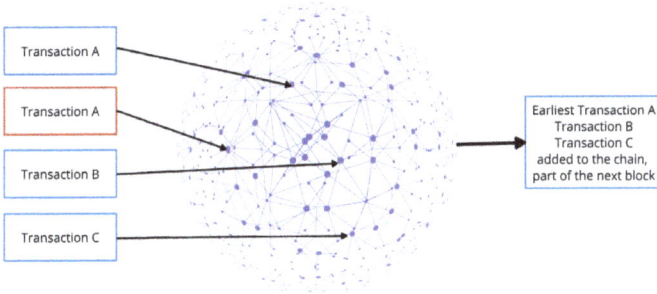

In a very large distributed network it is common for blocks to be created simultaneously, but only one will take its rightful place in the chain. Transactions that find themselves orphaned in unadopted blocks are simply added to the next available block. The process of agreeing on the longest (best) chain and updating the nodes is called a consensus mechanism.

CONSENSUS MECHANISMS

In Chapter 1 we talked about Proof of Work on the Bitcoin blockchain and Proof of Stake on Ethereum and other blockchains. These are the most high-profile examples of consensus mechanisms but there are others, notably Proof of Authority and Delegated Proof of Stake.

Byzantine Fault Tolerance

All consensus mechanisms are trying to achieve Byzantine Fault Tolerance (BFT). An agreed system state must be reached, in this case confirming that the new block is part of the longest chain and should be adopted by every node. However, not all nodes will be active when the block is added, and some nodes may be malicious.

By asking participants to invest resources in reaching a consensus, through mining or by locking their tokens in a staking pool, the probability of the right decision being made should outweigh that of acting on malicious messages (for example, adding a block with an invalid or criminal transaction). There are additional safeguards built in; for example in Proof of Stake, block validations are checked by a peer, and if the validator has tried to manipulate the result, their staked tokens are burned. BFT takes its name from the conceptual Byzantine Generals Problem which was devised in research supported by NASA to mitigate the impact of faulty processors on a large network (Lamport et al, 1982).

A consensus mechanism is an automated process that enables the network to agree that the chain should now include the newest block of transactions. As part of this process the block hash is generated, a new block is opened ready to be filled with the next batch of transactions, and the lucky 'winner' of the consensus process receives transaction fees and some newly minted coins that increase the supply of the chain's native cryptocurrency. Once consensus is reached, every node adopts the agreed chain. If a node is inactive, it will adopt the longest chain when next online.

To 'win' the consensus process, a user needs to be not just a node, but a full node. In Proof of Work, the full nodes are miners, competing for the prize. In Proof of Stake, pools of staked tokens delegate to full nodes who can be selected for validation. There is clear financial incentive, encouraging the public network to maintain the security of the chain.

The greatest danger for a blockchain is a 51% attack, a situation where a single entity gains control of the majority of full nodes. There are concerns that groups of miners or staking pools could amass enough voting or mining power to manipulate activity on the blockchain. Stakers are encouraged to choose smaller pools to minimise the likelihood of this happening, but the fewer the entities involved in consensus, the greater the risk.

The theft of $625 million from the bridge between the Ethereum and Ronin blockchains resulted from a 51% attack.

The bridge ran a Proof of Authority consensus mechanism with nine full nodes. Attackers gained access to one through a whitelisted account that had been left open, then compromised four more whose users were all part of the same organisation. With majority control, the attackers processed two fraudulent transactions that drained millions of dollars' worth of assets.

Figure 7.4 Common consensus mechanisms

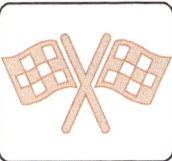

Proof of Work
- A constant race to solve the algorithm for every new proposed block.
- Miners must be the first to calculate a value of x that will generate a block hash with n leading zeros.
- This calculated value is called the *nonce* and forms part of the block header.

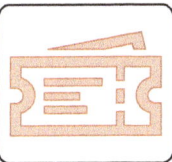

Proof of Stake
- Staking pools hold tokens contributed by many users.
- Pools are chosen at random to confirm a block, but the more tokens or multiples of the stake that they hold, the more chances they have.
- Delegated proof of stake divides pools into groups, making the process faster.

Proof of Authority
- Nodes are chosen to be part of the consensus mechanism. They could be individuals or corporations or any similar entity.
- A node is selected at random to confirm each block.
- The process is fast, but the fewer nodes there are, the higher the danger that bad actors could take control of a majority of nodes and process malicious transactions.

Network efficiency

All networks try to achieve a trade-off between Consistency, Availability and Partition tolerance (CAP). Blockchains are no exception. Every distributed system must have partition tolerance to ensure that it continues to operate even with data loss or system failure. Blockchains have eventual consistency and immediate availability, as data posted to the ledger is visible as soon as a transaction is validated. A key goal is to minimise latency, the time it takes for data to move between nodes, as low latency improves consistency and availability.

The measure of latency, block time, is the time required to generate the next block of transactions. Older chains and certain consensus mechanisms have higher latency. The Bitcoin blockchain takes ten minutes to generate each block and processes just seven transactions per second. The block time for Ethereum is approximately 12 seconds, processing 25 transactions per second. At the other end of the scale, Solana, using its high-volume architecture and novel Proof of History consensus mechanism, can process up to 60,000 transactions per second with a block time (slot time) of less than 0.4 seconds, and virtually instant settlement.

THE HONEST LEDGER

The consensus mechanism that closes each block and therefore renders transactions unchangeable gives us *trust* in the blockchain. The network of peer-to-peer nodes gives us a *decentralised* structure. The APIs from each blockchain allow every block and every transaction on a public blockchain to be viewed on a variety of block explorer websites, making the activity *transparent*. Figure 7.5 is an extract from the Etherscan website showing the most recent blocks and the most recent transactions confirmed within those blocks.

Figure 7.5 The honest ledger – data visible on a public blockchain

Latest Blocks			Latest Transactions		
Block Height	Txns	Time	Txn Hash	Type	Value
20106413	262	2024-02-23 14:07:24	e04ae1...926557	Commit	0 ETH
20106412	190	2024-02-23 14:07:14	1ed015...728e06	Approve	0 ETH
20106411	81	2024-02-23 14:07:01	454a4d...34b30a	Transfer	0.00872 ETH
20106410	248	2024-02-23 14:06:52	8b5898...275d1c	Mint	0.0025 ETH
20106409	106	2024-02-23 14:06:39	0af864...a53297	Swap	2.005 ETH
20106408	143	2024-02-23 14:06:30	dce8a1...3d52a3	Claim	0 ETH
20106407	197	2024-02-23 14:06:18	9ea1d1...b5c32e	Transfer	0.06443 ETH

Blockchain is an honest ledger of transactions and ownership. It can be trusted thanks to the structure and security of the chain, and the details of every action and every movement of assets are broadcast to the network, keeping people honest. As we saw in Chapter 4, using blockchain to secure decisions (Kraken IM) and gather prime entry data (Circulor) holds people to account and is changing behaviours.

In banking and business, however, activities require commercial confidentiality beyond that which is afforded by hashing transaction data. How can organisations take advantage of the trust and decentralisation of blockchain without compromising their privacy? The answer lies in defining exactly who needs access to the data, and a range of private (permissioned) blockchains have developed alongside their public counterparts to facilitate confidential applications.

PRIVATE DISTRIBUTED LEDGERS

In 2015, Ethereum was launched with smart contracts to automate functions and a layer above the blockchain for the development of software applications. In the same year, private (permissioned) blockchains made their appearance. The Linux Foundation launched the Hyperledger Project, an open-source collaboration of major multinationals including IBM. R3 Corda, the brainchild of bankers who needed tight access controls and high degrees of confidence alongside transparency and trust, emerged at the same time.

Ethereum is highly regarded as a technology, and it is possible to develop a permissioned Ethereum chain, for example that used in the World Food Programme's Building Blocks initiative. Application developers ConsenSys, led by Ethereum co-founder Joe Lubin, have also partnered with Hyperledger.

These private blockchains do not have cryptocurrencies, although they can have native crypto assets where the organisation needs them, for example to track the custody and condition of goods through a supply chain, or the use of parcels of funding, or to allocate a persistent identity to components.

The Hyperledger Project

This is an open-source operating system for marketplace, data sharing, micro-currencies and decentralised communities. It was developed to reduce security risks and ensure that access to transaction data remains with the parties involved. Initiated by IBM and the Linux Foundation, high-profile partners have included Accenture, ConsenSys, DTCC, Digital Asset, Fujitsu, Hitachi, IBM and JP Morgan Chase, although the exact make-up of the consortium varies over time. Hyperledger offers a pick-and-mix developer SDK with different distributed ledger frameworks and interoperable tools and libraries. Circulor's blockchain runs on Hyperledger as part of Oracle's software.

Its individual distributed ledgers are projects that have a specific purpose or structure. They include the following:

- Fabric – the original Hyperledger project led by IBM. It is a foundation for developing applications or solutions with a modular architecture, intended for enterprise use with channels of confidential data alongside a more open ledger for all participants. Oracle uses Hyperledger Fabric as the basis of its Blockchain Platform Cloud Service.

- Sawtooth – a modular platform for building, deploying and running distributed ledgers.

- Indy – provides tools, libraries and reusable components for creating and using independent digital identities.

- Iroha – aimed at helping businesses and financial institutions manage digital assets, written in C++.

- Besu – an open-source Ethereum client developed under the Apache 2.0 licence and written in Java.

R3 Corda

Founded in 2014 with a focus on financial services, R3 Corda is backed by a global banking consortium, initially with nine and now with more than sixty partners. The focus is on establishing digital trust between parties, and this is delivered by a permissioned chain with very tight access controls. Smart contracts can link to legal prose and the unique notary function ensures that transactions are not duplicated.

R3 Corda is the blockchain of choice for banking, fintech and insurtech projects. The Insurwave platform was built on Corda to protect highly confidential data. It is also popular in other sectors based on its robustness, security and pedigree. The AgriLedger blended finance platform runs on this blockchain.

Consensus without cryptocurrencies

Permissioned distributed ledgers have the same requirement as public blockchains to demonstrate Byzantine Fault Tolerance, but have to achieve it without a network of independent validators or paying cryptocurrency rewards.

A wide range of solutions have been developed. One of the earliest was Proof of Elapsed Time (PoET). This implements a lottery system, sending a message to every Intel chip in the network nodes to ask them to sleep for a random period of time. The first node to wake confirms the block. Others include

Tendermint, a consensus that is used by private ledgers and by the Cosmos public blockchain, Yet Another Consensus (YAC), which sits within the Iroha framework, and Apache Kafka.

Some are tied to a particular framework; others are interoperable and can be selected according to the best fit for the platform. If you are implementing a permissioned blockchain platform, the choice of consensus is part of the development process.

DO YOU REALLY NEED A BLOCKCHAIN?

Crypto and blockchain are tools for digital transformation and are a maturing part of the technology stack. Consider adding them to your toolkit if you want to fundamentally change how you operate and deliver value to your customers. They can be game changing for:

- business processes – both internal, such as supply chains, or outward facing, for example in customer relations and marketing

- business models, changing how value is delivered to customers, for example enabling digital ownership; this is a crucial element of the burgeoning Web3 economy

- developing new products and new markets, both physical and virtual

- organisations and culture, changing behaviours and increasing transparency and confidence.

Of course, as part of a wide range of very different emerging and established technologies, blockchain and crypto assets are not an appropriate solution for every problem. When the boom of token sales was in full swing, entrepreneurs tried to shoehorn blockchain into their business plans in order to raise money, whether by launching a cryptocurrency or NFT collection to the public, or to suggest to potential investors that they were innovative. This is possibly the worst reason to consider blockchain technology!

Figure 7.6 Do you really need a blockchain?

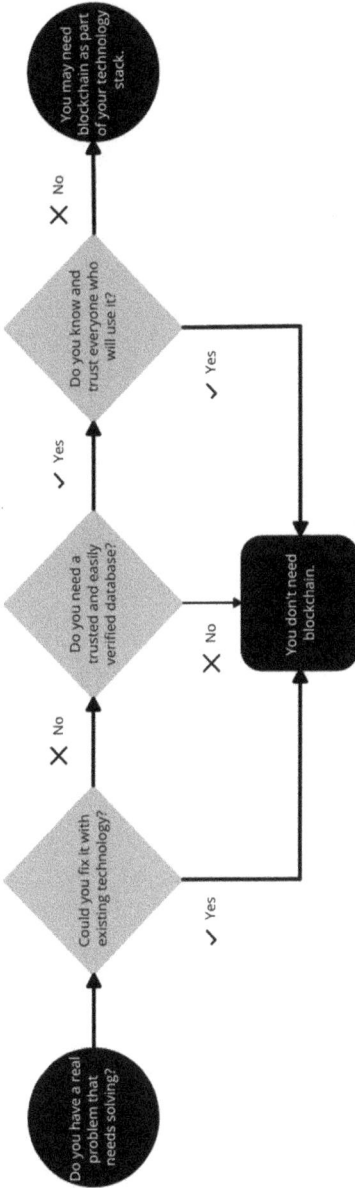

Identifying an existing pain point or a strong commercial strategy is the logical first step, and defining the appropriate technology stack to deliver what is needed is the second. It may or may not include blockchain.

In the next and final chapter, we will look towards the future of crypto and blockchain and some of the transformative ideas and projects that are emerging as the technology and the markets mature.

Chapter 7 Key takeaways

- Blockchain is simply a chain of blocks secured using cryptographic techniques.
- It is immutable, trusted and transparent.
- Blockchains may be public or private depending on the commercial requirements.

8 An Eye on the Future

Crypto assets and blockchain technology are finding their niches. The power of distributed, trusted and immutable records is only going to become greater as we try to make sense of the enormous volume of data being generated by our daily interactions with technology. Blockchain is already delivering the information we need to make effective decisions on supply chain management and sustainability reporting, and there will be more similar examples as time goes on.

Blockchain ensures that the data we gather from the increasingly sophisticated Internet of Things can be trusted and verified. Feeding trusted and transparent data to machine learning and deep learning algorithms can improve confidence in the output from AI models for effective decision-making support. Decentralised frameworks, NFTs and tokenisation are a fundamental part of Web3, adding ownership and trust to virtual industry and creative collaboration in the next iteration of the internet.

This exploits what we already know we can do with blockchain and crypto – but what lies in the future? Tokenisation of real-world assets (RWAs) is accelerating in different industries for different commercial reasons. DAOs are under scrutiny for their potential to deliver social impact where other decision-making structures have failed, and blockchain is already being put to good use in helping those in need, including in digital identity projects. Let's look at these two significant trends that may shape how we use blockchain and crypto in the coming decade.

TOKENISATION

Financial services and investment

An OECD report in 2020 suggested that asset tokenisation was already one of the best use-cases for blockchain in financial markets, mentioning financial instruments, baskets of collateral and physical assets (Nassr, 2020). Challenges at the time included scalability, settlement finality and network stability, all of which have been addressed by the development of newer, faster and more reliable blockchains. The EU's DLT Pilot Regime, introduced in 2023, allows market infrastructures to apply for authorisation to trade tokenised financial instruments on distributed ledger technology (DLT) platforms (Coraggio, Pantaleo and Gambula, 2023). Fully reserved stablecoins are effectively tokenised cash, and we've already seen tokens being used by JP Morgan on their Onyx platform (see Chapter 4) to speed up the movement of assets. This is starting to tip the balance into mainstream adoption.

Commodities and physical assets

Commodity tokenisation has been hailed as a safety net for crypto investors who want to diversify their portfolios in times of volatility (Tkachenko, 2022). This allows investors to earn from and trade a physical asset without ever taking custody of it, and wherever there is a commodity in limited supply, there is tokenisation. Jade City (2023) proposes, naturally, jade as the commodity of choice. Ubuntu Tribe tokenises gold, leveraging Africa's under-utilised natural resource and offering savings and investment opportunities to unbanked citizens (Orufa, 2023).

High-value physical assets are also being tokenised to offer financing and liquidity to owners. NFTs are already used as loan collateral in decentralised finance but the tokenisation of a physical item such as artwork allows ownership to be fractionalised for collateral and liquidity (Steves, 2023).

BLOCKCHAIN FOR GOOD

The United Nations saw the potential of blockchain and crypto assets very early on. A UN Joint Inspection Unit report (Dumitriu, 2020) recognised that blockchain carried 'unprecedented opportunities for inter-agency collaboration'. The report identified applications for distributed ledger technology in every one of the UN's 17 sustainable development goals and made a series of recommendations including supporting the creation of a United Nations digital identity. Projects running at that time included livestock traceability in Papua New Guinea, the Building Blocks programme supporting refugees in Jordan and Bangladesh, and notarisation of documents to prove ownership of parcels of land.

In 2023, the UNHCR won an award for its project using blockchain technology to disburse cash to people displaced by the war in Ukraine. The pilot, supported by the Stellar Development Foundation, used a secure smartphone wallet to issue USDC stablecoins to eligible claimants which could then be converted to fiat currencies at any MoneyGram location (UNHCR, 2022).

A current UNICEF innovation is the Giga programme, mapping school internet access in real time. By providing reliable data, several countries including Kyrgyzstan and Rwanda succeeding in negotiating better services, reducing costs and attracting investment to improve access to education.

An independent project, World Mobile, is also addressing connectivity, building a blockchain-based mobile network in hard-to-reach places. It's estimated that almost three billion people are unconnected, losing out on economic, health and social opportunities. The first phase of World Mobile's deployment connected 20,000 citizens on Zanzibar for the first time. Every transmitter is a node on the network, attracting small parcels of capital investment from communities and individuals, and rewarding the owner (World Mobile, 2023).

Distributed Autonomous Organisations

A report by the World Economic Forum in 2023 on Impact DAOs says that although nascent and aspirational, they are already driving change and revealing insights about the future of social impact (WEF, 2023). Examples highlighted include:

- Ukraine DAO, that has donated more than $7 million to specific causes supporting the armed forces and the LGBT community, and a project documenting evidence of war crimes
- Gitcoin, a philanthropic DAO that has funded almost 4,000 projects from 3.8 million unique donations, choosing the recipients through community voting
- Kolektivo, a small DAO that issues micro grants to community projects.

The governance of DAOs remains a problem, with no minimum number of token holders required, so centralisation is inevitable in the early days, and no clear template for an effective voting structure. However, we can expect to see the use of DAOs increasing.

Cryptocurrency use

Although it is unusual for cryptocurrencies to be used directly for goods and services, there are exceptions. In September 2021, El Salvador recognised Bitcoin as legal tender, adopting the cryptocurrency alongside the US Dollar. El Salvador has no native currency and every monetary policy decision taken in Washington affected the country regardless of its economic situation. The influences driving adoption were complex, with Bitcoin enthusiasts first setting up an entire town, El Zonte, as a closed Bitcoin economy and courting the young president, Nayib Bukele.

The rollout of Bitcoin met with resistance, but there were incentives for citizens to set up the new Chivo wallet for Bitcoin and US Dollar transactions and fast cross-border payments. A report by the International Monetary Fund suggested that soon after launch there were 3.8 million active Chivo wallets (IMF, 2022) in a country that has limited access to traditional banking services, which is a cautious success story, despite issues with fraudulent use of ID documents when setting them up. Since then, there has been some investment in infrastructure, new services established such as a veterinary clinic that takes Bitcoin, and exploration of clean mining using geothermal energy. There are still plenty of concerns about the long-term impact on El Salvador's economy, but it is one to watch.

Digital identity

Up to 1.5 billion people in the world have no official identity. Identity is the gateway to government services, education, participation in the economy and financial inclusion, among other things. Development initiatives are running across the world including some African countries, India, and with refugees through the United Nations. Blockchain is at the heart of establishing a unique digital identity. At the basic level it simply involves taking a biometric and hashing it up onto a blockchain, as the World Food Programme did with Building Blocks, but the problem is portability of that identity as refugees are resettled. Government agencies across the world need to treat digital identities as interoperable with existing systems of identification and certification.

WHERE DO WE GO FROM HERE?

Interest in crypto assets and blockchains is showing no signs of diminishing, despite volatility in the market, and the scandals and scams that beset the industry. Legislation and regulation are beginning to crystallise around crypto activities, and this can only be positive.

Maturing, rapid and sustainable technology is allowing every industry to use blockchain and crypto assets where appropriate to solve real problems. The distributed structure of blockchain opens up new ways of operating and there is an increasing focus on making the world better for everyone.

We are entering a time when the technology will take second place to the impact of a project. Soon, we will neither know nor care whether the transaction we just completed or the good cause we supported involves blockchain or crypto assets, in the same way that we pay scant attention to TCP/IP protocols underneath our internet communications, or the AI algorithms that personalise our lives.

In this golden period of conscious innovation, it is up to us to realise the benefits and mitigate the risks in order to make the most of crypto assets and blockchain.

Final takeaways

- Your family, employees, colleagues, clients and suppliers may already be using crypto and blockchain. This book should help you to help them avoid risks and reap benefits.

- Not your keys, not your crypto! Be aware of criminals. Crypto assets are valuable and fraudulent schemes are clever. Do your own research to verify claims and promises. If it looks too good to be true, it probably is.

- Familiarise yourself with the current legislation and regulations in your jurisdiction for crypto and blockchain activities, accounting, taxation, insurance, legacy planning and other legal matters.

- Think outside the box. Blockchain offers new collaborative and economic models that can drive change.

Abbreviations

AML	Anti-money laundering
API	Application programming interface
BTC	The Bitcoin blockchain's native token
CBDC	Central Bank Digital Currency
CFTC	Commodity Futures Trading Commission (US)
CTF	Counter-Terrorism Financing
CPU	Central processing unit
DAO	Distributed (or Decentralised) Autonomous Organisation
DLT	Distributed ledger technology
ESG	Environmental, Social and Governance
ETH	The Ethereum blockchain's native token
FASB	Financial Accounting Standards Board
FATF	Financial Action Task Force
FCA	Financial Conduct Authority (UK)
FSB	Financial Stability Board
FSCS	Financial Services Compensation Scheme
FOMO	Fear of Missing Out
GDPR	General Data Protection Regulation
KYC	Know Your Customer
LLM	Large language model (for example, ChatGPT)
LINK	The Chainlink blockchain's native token
MiCA	The EU's Markets in Crypto-Assets Regulation 2023

MLR The UK's Money Laundering, Terrorist Financing and Transfer of Funds (Information on the Payer) Regulations 2017

NFT Non-fungible token

PSR Payment Service Regulator (UK)

SEC Securities and Exchange Commission (US)

XRP The Ripple blockchain's native token

Glossary

51% attack: A malicious actor taking control of a majority of blockchain validators.

Airdrop: Unsolicited receipt of a token which may be expected, benign or malicious.

Altcoin: A cryptocurrency other than Bitcoin.

Anti-money laundering (AML): Global regulatory requirement for financial services.

Bear market: A period of falling asset values and low confidence.

Biometrics: Security features using 'what you are' – fingerprint, voiceprint, face.

Bitcoin: The first cryptocurrency and its blockchain.

Block explorer: A public browser representation of blockchain activity.

Block hash: The cryptographic signature of the entire contents of a block in the chain.

Block height: The position of a block in the chain; its height above the genesis block.

Block reward: Coins added to the supply when a block is closed and the next opened.

Block time: The time between blocks, determining the latency of the chain.

Blockchain: Blocks of timestamped transactions linked by a distributed cryptographic chain.

Bull run: A period of rising market values and high confidence.

Checksum: Automatic detection of errors, for example detecting an invalid wallet address.

Cold wallet: A storage medium for private wallet keys that is kept offline.

Consensus mechanism: A software protocol that enables a distributed network to agree on its state, even if some nodes are offline or faulty. In the case of blockchain, it is an agreement to add a new block to the chain.

Crypto (1): Abbreviation of 'cryptographic', which means secured using cryptography. Cryptographic assets are known as crypto assets; cryptographic currency as cryptocurrency.

Crypto (2): An abbreviation that may be used to describe the industry of crypto assets or crypto assets themselves.

Crypto assets: Software tokens on a blockchain whose functions are programmable and which can be owned. They may be fungible or non-fungible.

Cryptocurrency: Fungible crypto assets or tokens.

Custodian: An organisation or individual holding assets or private keys granting access to assets on behalf of the owner. Some crypto exchanges are custodians.

Decentraland: A decentralised virtual world on the Ethereum blockchain.

Decentralised exchange: An automated cryptocurrency exchange where liquidity is provided by a community of users in return for exchange fees.

Digital asset: A crypto asset. The term is most commonly, but not exclusively, used to describe non-fungible tokens, and is often more palatable for business use.

Distributed Autonomous Organisation (DAO): A blockchain-based organisation where decisions are taken by the community of token holders.

Distributed ledger technology (DLT): A network that uses the resources of many nodes to ensure data security and transparency. Blockchain is a subset of distributed ledger technology.

Dogecoin: An early cryptocurrency with little utility.

Ethereum: The second largest cryptocurrency and blockchain after Bitcoin.

Exchange: A platform where value held in one cryptocurrency can be converted to another, and in some cases to and from fiat currency.

Fiat currency: Central bank money; money that is not cryptocurrency.

Fungibility: An economic property whereby every unit and sub-unit of an asset can be freely exchanged for another of the same asset, for example pounds sterling and pence.

Gas fee: A transaction fee on the Ethereum network based on the functions executed in the transaction and a variable tariff for network congestion.

Genesis block: The very first block in a chain.

Hard wallet: A physical storage medium for private wallet keys, normally kept offline.

Hashing: The process of assigning a numeric or alphanumeric string to a piece of data.

Hot wallet: A storage application for private wallet keys that is online.

Immutable: Unchangeable.

Key logging: A piece of malware that records the keystrokes on a computer keyboard, used to try and capture login credentials.

Key pair: A private and a public key; security credentials used to prove your identity and interact with a blockchain.

Latency: The degree of delay on a distributed system as data moves between nodes.

Malware: Malicious software introduced onto a computer or smart device to execute operations such as key logging, ransomware or cloning authentication tools.

Merkle root: The digital fingerprint of all the transactions held in a single block.

MetaMask: A popular browser-based wallet for Ethereum and related blockchains.

Mining: The process of calculating the algorithm for each block hash in the hope of being the first to succeed and receive the block reward.

Minting: The process of creating a crypto asset on a blockchain.

Mnemonic phrase: A 12- or 24-word phrase that can be used to recover the private key of a crypto wallet. It is provided to the user when a wallet is created and must be kept securely or access to assets can be lost.

Native cryptocurrency: A cryptocurrency that is part of the operational code of its blockchain; for example, Bitcoin on the Bitcoin blockchain, XRP on the Ripple blockchain.

Node: An entity connected to a blockchain as part of the distributed network.

Non-fungible: An asset that is unique and indivisible.

Oracle: A source of data recorded on a blockchain.

Partition tolerance: The tolerance of a distributed system to network failures.

Permissioned blockchain: A blockchain with access controls, likely to be a private chain with no native cryptocurrency.

Privacy chain: A public blockchain designed to obfuscate transaction details and wallet addresses for all but the parties to the transaction. This ensures anonymity (rather than pseudonymity) for users.

Private key: The cryptographic signature required to interact with your owned assets on a blockchain. It must be kept securely or access to assets can be lost. It cannot be regenerated under any circumstance but can be recovered using its mnemonic phrase.

Proof of Authority: A consensus mechanism using votes from a limited population of authorised nodes.

Proof of Stake: A consensus mechanism using votes from nodes to which token holders have delegated their voting power.

Proof of Work: A consensus mechanism using computer processing power to compete in calculating an algorithm.

Pseudonymity: Being identified by an alias, or pseudonym. On a blockchain the pseudonym is a wallet address. All blockchains other than privacy chains are pseudonymous, not anonymous, and the real identity behind a wallet address can be discovered.

Public key: The address of your wallet on a blockchain to which assets can be sent. It is visible on a block explorer.

Ransomware: Malware that permanently blocks access to the victim's data or entire computer network unless a ransom is paid.

Rug pull: A type of crypto scam where the creators of an asset (often an NFT) use heavy marketing and influencer activity to hype investment, then disappear with the funds.

Satoshi: The pseudonymous inventor of Bitcoin. The atomic unit of Bitcoin; 100 million Satoshis equal one Bitcoin.

Security token: A crypto asset that is offered for sale to raise investment and in doing so is judged by securities regulators to be akin to a share in the company rather than a token with future utility.

Self-custody: Holding the private key to a crypto wallet, as distinct from trusting a third party with custodianship.

Smart contract: A computer program automating functions on a blockchain that follows 'if this then that' logic. Not smart, not usually contracts.

Social engineering: Psychological manipulation techniques used by cybercriminals and fraudsters aimed at talking a target into performing a specific action for illegitimate reasons.

Stablecoin: A special class of cryptocurrency whose value is pegged to that of a real-world commodity or fiat currency.

Staking: The process of locking tokens into the consensus mechanism of a Proof of Stake blockchain in exchange for rewards.

Staking pool: A pool of funds that collectively earns block validation rewards in a Proof of Stake consensus mechanism.

Token: A discrete item of code programmed to work within a software application. Tokens that work within a blockchain are also known as crypto assets or digital assets.

Utility token: A crypto asset that may be offered for sale to raise investment based on its future utility and value within the software that is being developed.

Wallet: An application or device that is accessed using a private key and enables the owner to send, receive and use their crypto assets.

References

Adachi, M., Da Silva, P., Born, A., Cappuccio, M, Czák-Ludwig, S., Gschossmann. I., Paula, G., Pellicani, A., Philipps, S-M., Plooij, M., Rossteuscher, I. and Zeoli, P. (2022) Stablecoins' role in crypto and beyond: functions, risks and policy. European Central Bank. Available from https://www.ecb.europa.eu/pub/financial-stability/macroprudential-bulletin/html/ecb.mpbu202207_2~836f682ed7.en.html

Aju, M. and Burrell, T. (2023) Research note: Cryptoassets consumer research 2023 (Wave 4). Financial Conduct Authority. Available from https://www.fca.org.uk/publication/research-notes/research-note-cryptoasset-consumer-research-2023-wave4.pdf

Atlantic Council (2023) Central Bank Digital Currency tracker. Available from https://www.atlanticcouncil.org/cbdctracker/

Bank of England (2017) FinTech accelerator proof of concept. Available from https://www.bankofengland.co.uk/-/media/boe/files/fintech/ripple.pdf

Banque de France (2023) Wholesale CBDC: as decisive as Retail CBDC, and actively experimenting. Speech by François Villeroy de Galhau, Governor of the Banque de France at the conference "Unveiling the potential of wholesale CBDC: what insights and prospects?" Available from https://www.banque-france.fr/en/governors-interventions/wholesale-cbdc-decisive-retail-cbdc-and-actively-experimenting

Baucherel, K. (2020) *Blockchain hurricane: origins, applications and future of blockchain and cryptocurrency.* New York: Business Expert Press, pp.60–61.

Beganski, A. (2023) NFT Trader accidentally burns $129K CryptoPunk. Decrypt. Available from https://decrypt.co/124598/nft-trader-accidentally-burns-129k-cryptopunk

Bentley (2022) Bentley announces the release of a limited genesis NFT created by Bentley designers. Available from https://www.bentleymotors.com/en/world-of-bentley/news/2022-news/bentley-enters-nft-marketplace-with-limited-nft.html

BIS Innovation Hub (2023) Project mBridge: experimenting with a multi-CBDC platform for cross-border payments. Available from https://www.bis.org/about/bisih/topics/cbdc/mcbdc_bridge.htm

Bloomberg Law (2022). Cryptocurrency laws and regulations by state. Available from https://pro.bloomberglaw.com/brief/cryptocurrency-laws-and-regulations-by-state

Browning, S. and Codd, F. (2023) Regulation of cryptocurrency. House of Commons Library. Available from https://researchbriefings.files.parliament.uk/documents/CDP-2023-0018/CDP-2023-0018.pdf

Campbell, P. (2020) EV supply chains seek clearer visibility with blockchain. *Financial Times*. Available from https://www.ft.com/content/3652b68e-206f-4e3a-9b3a-4d5ec9a285b7

CFTC (2024) Digital assets. Commodity Futures Trading Commission. Available from https://www.cftc.gov/digitalassets/index.htm

Chainalysis (2023) Lessons from $11 billion in recovered cryptocurrency: the industry needs proper incident response. Chainalysis. Available from https://www.chainalysis.com/blog/crypto-needs-proper-incident-response

Chinwe M. (2024) Nigeria, 19 other countries gain USDC access as Coinbase partners Yellow Card. BusinessDay. Available from https://businessday.ng/technology/article/nigeria-19-other-countries-gain-usdc-access-as-coinbase-partners-yellow-card/

Coraggio, G., Pantaleo, A. and Gambula, E. (2023) Tokenization of financial instruments and the new legal framework in EU: the DLT Pilot Regime and ESMA guidelines. DLA Piper. Available from https://www.dlapiper.com/en/insights/publications/2023/04/tokenization-of-financial-instruments-and-the-new-legal-framework-in-eu

Court of Justice of the European Union (2015) The Court of Justice declares that the Commission's US Safe Harbour Decision is invalid. Judgment in Case C-362/14 Maximillian Schrems v Data Protection Commissioner. Available from https://curia.europa.eu/jcms/upload/docs/application/pdf/2015-10/cp150117en.pdf#:~:text=Mr%20Schrems%20lodged%20a%20complaint,'the%20NSA'))%2C%20the

Crawford, S. (2023) Digitising maritime insurance risk. Insurwave. Available from https://insurwave.com/blog/insights/digitising-maritime-insurance-risk

Cross, M. (2023) Digital assets: call for legislation to protect third category of 'thing'. The Law Society Gazette. Available from https://www.lawgazette.co.uk/law/digital-assets-call-for-legislation-to-protect-third-category-of-thing-/5116458.article

CryptoCurrencyWire (2023) JPMorgan report shows crypto miners are diversifying business interests. Available from https://www.cryptocurrencywire.com/jpmorgan-report-shows-crypto-miners-are-diversifying-business-interests

de Vries, A. (2023) Cryptocurrencies on the road to sustainability: Ethereum paving the way for Bitcoin. Patterns. Available from https://doi.org/10.1016/j.patter.2022.100633

del Castillo, M. (2015) The 'Great Bitcoin Exodus' has totally changed New York's bitcoin ecosystem. *New York Business Journal*. Available from https://www.bizjournals.com/newyork/news/2015/08/12/the-great-bitcoin-exodus-has-totally-changed-new.html

Decentraland (2023) Tradition and innovation collide: Decentraland Metaverse Fashion Week 2023. Available from https://decentraland.org/blog/announcements/tradition-and-innovation-collide-decentraland-metaverse-fashion-week-2023

Detrio, C. (2017) EIP-779: Hardfork Meta: DAO Fork. Ethereum Improvement Proposals. Available from https://eips.ethereum.org/EIPS/eip-779

Digiconomist (2024) Ethereum Energy Consumption Index. Available from https://digiconomist.net/ethereum-energy-consumption

Dowlat, S. (2018) Cryptoasset market coverage initiation: network creation, pp.23–25. Available from https://research.bloomberg.com/pub/res/d28giW28tf6G7T_Wr77aU0gDgFQ

Dumitriu, P. (2020) Blockchain applications in the United Nations system: towards a state of readiness, pp.7, 71–76. United Nations. Available from https://www.unjiu.org/sites/www.unjiu.org/files/jiu_rep_2020_7_english.pdf

Ethereum (2014) Introduction to smart contracts. Ethereum Whitepaper. Available from https://ethereum.org/en/smart-contracts/#introduction-to-smart-contracts

Ethereum (2023) How to revoke smart contract access to your crypto funds. Available from https://ethereum.org/en/guides/how-to-revoke-token-access

European Commission (2024) Data Act. Available from https://digital-strategy.ec.europa.eu/en/policies/data-act

FASB (2024) Accounting for and Disclosure of Crypto Assets. Financial Accounting Standards Board. Available from https://www.fasb.org/page/PageContent?pageId=/projects/recentlycompleted/accounting-for-and-disclosure-of-crypto-assets.html

FATF (2023) Virtual assets. Financial Action Task Force. Available from https://www.fatf-gafi.org/en/topics/virtual-assets.html

FCA (2023) PS23/6: Financial promotion rules for cryptoassets. Financial Conduct Authority. Available from https://www.fca.org.uk/publication/policy/ps23-6.pdf

FCA Innovation Hub (2023) Regulatory Sandbox. Financial Conduct Authority. Available from https://www.fca.org.uk/firms/innovation/regulatory-sandbox

FCA InvestSmart (2024) Crypto: The basics. Financial Conduct Authority. Available from https://www.fca.org.uk/investsmart/crypto-basics

Fearn, A. Saunders, C. and Kantar Public (2022) Individuals holding cryptoassets: uptake and understanding. HMRC. Available from https://www.gov.uk/government/publications/individuals-holding-cryptoassets-uptake-and-understanding

Financial Conduct Authority (2022a) Hype – spot the signs and manage your FOMO. Available from https://www.fca.org.uk/investsmart/hype-spot-signs-manage-your-fomo

Financial Conduct Authority (2022b) Warning: FTX. Available from https://www.fca.org.uk/news/warnings/ftx

Fleming, T., Passmore, M., Kan, M., Howell, M. and Bautista-Beauchesne, N. (2022) Ontario Securities Commission Crypto Asset Survey. Available from https://www.osc.ca/sites/default/files/2022-10/inv_research_20220928_crypto-asset-survey_EN.pdf

Franjkovic, T. (2023) UK Crypto Register: Full list of Financial Conduct Authority-Approved Firms. CCN. Available from https://www.ccn.com/crypto-register-fca-uk-list-approved-firms/

FSB (2023) High-level recommendations for the regulation, supervision and oversight of global stablecoin arrangements. Financial Stability Board. Available from https://www.fsb.org/2023/07/high-level-recommendations-for-the-regulation-supervision-and-oversight-of-global-stablecoin-arrangements-final-report/

Gibraltar Laws (2017) Financial Services (Distributed Ledger Technology Providers) Regulations 2017. Gibraltar Financial Services (Investment and Fiduciary Services). Available from https://www.gibraltarlaws.gov.gi/legislations/financial-services-distributed-ledger-technology-providers-regulations-2017-4218/download

Global Government Fintech (2022) Bahamas central bank shares CBDC lessons from Sand Dollar's first two years. Available from https://www.globalgovernmentfintech.com/bahamas-central-bank-cbdc-sand-dollar-first-two-years

Grobys, K. and Huynh, T. L. D. (2022) When Tether says "JUMP!" Bitcoin asks "How low?" *Finance Research Letters*, Volume 47, Part A, 102644. Available from https://doi.org/10.1016/j.frl.2021.102644

Guest, P. (2023) Bitcoin mining was booming in Kazakhstan. Then it was gone. *MIT Technology Review*. Available from https://www.technologyreview.com/2023/01/12/1066589/bitcoin-mining-boom-kazakhstan

Hackitt, J. (2018) Building a safer future – independent review of building regulations and fire safety: final report, pp.101–106. HM Government. Available from https://assets.publishing.service.gov.uk/media/5afc50c840f0b622e4844ab4/Building_a_Safer_Future_-_web.pdf

HM Government (2023) Factsheet: cryptoassets – legislation. Available from https://www.gov.uk/government/publications/economic-crime-and-corporate-transparency-bill-2022-factsheets/fact-sheet-cryptoassets-legislation

HM Treasury (2022) Government sets out plan to make UK a global cryptoasset technology hub. Available from https://www.gov.uk/government/news/government-sets-out-plan-to-make-uk-a-global-cryptoasset-technology-hub

HMRC (2024a) Cryptoassets manual. HM Revenue and Customs. Available from https://www.gov.uk/hmrc-internal-manuals/cryptoassets-manual

HMRC (2024b) Cryptoassets manual – Compliance: regulation and anti-money laundering. HM Revenue and Customs. Available from https://www.gov.uk/hmrc-internal-manuals/cryptoassets-manual/crypto100350

Hoffman, C. and Patel, D. (2023) Trade finance gap rises to $2.5 trillion USD. Trade Finance Global. Available from https://www.tradefinanceglobal.com/posts/trade-finance-gap-rises-to-2-5-trillion-usd-five-key-takeaways-adbs-latest-report-trade-finance-gaps-growth-jobs

IFRS (2023) General Sustainability-related Disclosures. Available from https://www.ifrs.org/projects/completed-projects/2023/general-sustainability-related-disclosures

Illgner, A. (2023) Swift and Chainlink's tokenised asset experiment. The Banker. Available from https://www.thebanker.com/Swift-and-Chainlink-s-tokenised-asset-experiment-1695022142

IMF (2022) El Salvador Country Report. International Monetary Fund. Available from https://www.imf.org/en/Publications/CR/Issues/2022/01/26/El-Salvador-2021-Article-IV-Consultation-Press-Release-Staff-Report-and-Statement-by-the-512245

IOSCO (2023) Policy recommendations for crypto and digital asset markets consultation report. International Organization of Securities Commissions. Available from https://www.iosco.org/library/pubdocs/pdf/IOSCOPD734.pdf

Issam, H. (2023) Non-EU countries' regulations on crypto-assets and their potential implications for the EU. European Parliament Briefing. Available from https://www.europarl.europa.eu/thinktank/en/document/EPRS_BRI(2023)753930

Jade City (2023) Pioneering real asset tokenisation with jade. Available from https://jadecity.io/docs/Jade-City-Litepaper.pdf

Jones, H. (2023) EU watchdog sets out capital, liquidity rules for stablecoin issuers. Reuters. Available from https://www.reuters.com/markets/europe/eu-watchdog-sets-out-capital-liquidity-rules-stablecoin-issuers-2023-11-08/

JP Morgan (2023) Settle repo transactions in minutes using blockchain. Available from https://www.jpmorgan.com/onyx/digital-financing

Kamsky, A. (2023) How Bitcoin pizza revolutionized cryptocurrency transactions. Cryptocurrency News. Available from https://www.ccn.com/how-bitcoin-pizza-revolutionized-cryptocurrency-transactions/

KPMG (2018) 2017 global venture capital investment hits decade high of US$155 billion following a strong Q4. KPMG Venture Pulse. Available from https://kpmg.com/sg/en/home/media/press-releases/2018/01/kpmg-venture-pulse-q4-2017.html

Lal, A., Zhu, J. and You, F. (2023) From mining to mitigation: How Bitcoin can support renewable energy development and climate action. American Chemical Society: ACS Sustainable Chem. Eng. 2023, 11, 45, 16330–16340. Available from https://doi.org/10.1021/acssuschemeng.3c05445

Lamport, L., Shostak, R. and Pease, M. (1982) The Byzantine Generals Problem. ACM Transactions on Programming Languages and Systems: Volume 4, Issue 3, July, pp.382–401. Available from https://doi.org/10.1145/357172.357176

Law Commission (2023) Digital assets: final report. Available from https://lawcom.gov.uk/project/digital-assets/

Law Library of Congress (2018) Regulation of cryptocurrency in selected jurisdictions. Available from https://tile.loc.gov/storage-services/service/ll/llglrd/2018298388/2018298388.pdf

Levy, J., de Tommaso, M. and Wilde, L. (2023) High Court allows service exclusively by NFT. Ashurst. Available from https://www.ashurst.com/en/insights/high-court-allows-service-exclusively-by-nft/

Li, J., Kassem, M. and Watson, R. (2020). A proposed framework for blockchain and smart contract-based automation of maintenance and repairs during operation of built assets. In Proc. 37th CIB W78 Information Technology for Construction Conference (CIB W78), São Paulo, Brazil, pp.347–362. Available from http://dx.doi.org/10.46421/2706-6568.37.2020.paper025

Long, C. (2019) What do Wyoming's 13 new Blockchain laws mean? Forbes. Available from https://www.forbes.com/sites/caitlinlong/2019/03/04/what-do-wyomings-new-blockchain-laws-mean

Lopez, E. (2022) Maersk, IBM to shut down blockchain joint venture TradeLens. Supply Chain Dive. Available from https://www.supplychaindive.com/news/Maersk-IBM-shut-down-TradeLens/637580/

Mattke, J., Maier, C. and Reis, L. (2020) Is cryptocurrency money? Three empirical studies analyzing medium of exchange, store of value and unit of account. In Proceedings of the 2020 on

Computers and People Research Conference (SIGMIS-CPR'20). Association for Computing Machinery, New York, NY, USA, 26–35. Available from https://doi.org/10.1145/3378539.3393859

May, T. (1988) The crypto anarchist manifesto. Available from https://nakamotoinstitute.org/crypto-anarchist-manifesto/

Mersetzky, M. (2023) Zug is the number one global crypto hub. Switzerland Global Enterprise. Available from https://www.s-ge.com/en/article/news/20232-crypto-global-crypto-hub-zug

MiCA (2023) Regulation (EU) 2023/1114 of the European Parliament and of the Council of 31 May 2023 on markets in crypto-assets, and amending Regulations (EU) No 1093/2010 and (EU) No 1095/2010 and Directives 2013/36/EU and (EU) 2019/1937. Available from https://eur-lex.europa.eu/legal-content/EN/TXT/HTML/?uri=CELEX:32023R1114

Middleton, J. (2023) Robot dogs, AI and the plan to retrieve £165m crypto fortune lost in rubbish dump. *The Independent*. Available from https://www.independent.co.uk/news/uk/home-news/lost-bitcoin-crypto-james-howells-b2406517.html

MIT Technology Review (2019) Mt. Gox was riddled with price manipulation, data mining reveals. Available from https://www.technologyreview.com/2019/02/21/1299/mt-gox-was-riddled-with-price-manipulation-data-mining-reveals

Murphy, H. and Stacey, K. (2022) Facebook Libra: the inside story of how the company's cryptocurrency dream died. *Financial Times*. Available from https://www.ft.com/content/a88fb591-72d5-4b6b-bb5d-223adfb893f3

Nakamoto, S. (2008) Bitcoin: A peer-to-peer electronic cash system. Available from https://galiadigital.co.uk/wp-content/uploads/2021/11/Satoshi-White-Paper-2008.pdf

Nassr, I.K. (2020) The tokenisation of assets and potential implications for financial markets. OECD. Available from https://web-archive.oecd.org/2020-01-17/542780-The-Tokenisation-of-Assets-and-Potential-Implications-for-Financial-Markets-HIGHLIGHTS.pdf

Noonan, L., Oliver, J. and Venkataramakrishnan, S. (2022) FCA extends crypto registration deadline for 12 firms in U-turn. *Financial Times*. Available from https://www.ft.com/content/20f57405-957d-46c2-88e2-266dae862fb9

NYDFS (2023) Virtual currency businesses guidance. New York State Department of Financial Services. Available from https://www.dfs.ny.gov/industry_guidance/industry_letters/il20230918_guidance_vc_listing

O'Connor, T. (2023) FCA issues 146 alerts on first day of crypto marketing rules. FT Adviser. Available from https://www.ftadviser.com/regulation/2023/10/10/fca-issues-146-alerts-on-first-day-of-crypto-marketing-rules/

O'Dwyer, M., Asgari, N. and Pickard, J. (2023) Former FCA boss warns of risks to investors from UK plan to regulate crypto. Financial Times. Available from https://www.ft.com/content/723b5753-06e1-4cd8-a629-dd795f9068f2

Open Access Government (2019) World Bank blockchain pilot sows fresh narrative for Haiti's farmers. Available from https://www.openaccessgovernment.org/world-bank-blockchain-haitis-farmers/61205/

OpenSea (2023) Coca-Cola. Available from https://opensea.io/Coca-Cola/activity

Orufa, S. (2023) How Ubuntu Tribe is unlocking Africa's gold wealth with blockchain. Ventures Africa. Available from https://venturesafrica.com/how-gift-is-unlocking-africas-gold-wealth-with-blockchain/

Plante, E. (2022) $30 Million seized: how the cryptocurrency community is making it difficult for North Korean hackers to profit. Chainalysis. Available from https://www.chainalysis.com/blog/axie-infinity-ronin-bridge-dprk-hack-seizure/

Pollman, E. (2023) Startup Failure. Duke Law Journal, Vol. 73, p. 327, U of Penn, Inst for Law & Econ Research Paper No. 23–31, European Corporate Governance Institute – Law Working Paper No. 729/2023. Available from https://papers.ssrn.com/sol3/papers.cfm?abstract_id=4535089

PR Newswire (2017) Propy announces world's first real estate purchase on Ethereum Blockchain. Available from https://www.prnewswire.com/news-releases/propy-announces-worlds-first-real-estate-purchase-on-ethereum-blockchain-300529474.html

PSG (2023) PSG Matchday Collection. Paris Saint-German. Available from https://en.psgmatchdaycollection.com

Rashid, A., Bakry, W. & Al-Mohamad, S. (2023) Are cryptocurrencies a future safe haven for investors? The case of Bitcoin. Economic Research-Ekonomska Istraživanja. Available from https://doi.org/10.1080/1331677X.2022.2140443

Reserve Bank of Australia (2023) Australian CBDC Pilot for Digital Finance Innovation. Available from https://www.rba.gov.au/payments-and-infrastructure/central-bank-digital-currency/pdf/australian-cbdc-pilot-for-digital-finance-innovation-project-report.pdf

Santander (2018) Santander launches the first blockchain-based international money transfer service across four countries. Available from https://www.santander.co.uk/about-santander/media-centre/press-releases/santander-launches-the-first-blockchain-based-international-money-transfer-service-across-four

Sarkar, A. (2022) AMM protocol SudoRare disappears from the internet with 519 ETH. CoinTelegraph. Available from https://cointelegraph.com/news/amm-protocol-sudorare-disappears-from-the-internet-with-519-eth

SEC (2024) Crypto assets. U.S. Securities and Exchange Commission. Available from https://www.investor.gov/additional-resources/spotlight/crypto-assets

Sharma, T., Zhou, Z., Miller, A. and Wang, Y. (2022) Exploring security practices of smart contract developers. Available from https://doi.org/10.48550/arXiv.2204.11193

Short, M., Baucherel, K., Rahimian, F., Joneidy, S., Adu-Amankwa, N.A., Parniani, B., Roughan, A. and Arutyunyan, A. (2022) Digital trade technology and policy – barriers and opportunities: A scoping report for a Centre for Digital Trade and Innovation. Teesside University. Available from https:// research.tees.ac.uk/en/publications/digital-trade-technology-and-policy-barriers-and-opportunities-a-

Small, Z. (2023) Hermès wins MetaBirkins lawsuit; jurors not convinced NFTs are art. *New York Times*. Available from https:// www.nytimes.com/2023/02/08/arts/hermes-metabirkins-lawsuit-verdict.html

Sotheby's (2021) Natively digital: A curated NFT sale / Lot 2. Available from https://www.sothebys.com/en/buy/ auction/2021/natively-digital-a-curated-nft-sale-2/quantum

Statista (2024) Number of cryptocurrencies worldwide from 2013 to August 2023. Available from https://www.statista. com/statistics/863917/number-crypto-coins-tokens/

Stempel, J. (2022) After 14 years, Lehman Brothers' brokerage ends liquidation. Reuters. Available from https://www. reuters.com/markets/us/after-14-years-lehman-brothers-brokerage-ends-liquidation-2022-09-28/

Steves, R. (2023) AllianceBlock partners with ARTBANX to make art a bankable asset class on blockchain. FinanceFeeds. Available from https://financefeeds.com/allianceblock-partners-with-artbanx-to-make-art-a-bankable-asset-class-on-blockchain/

Szabo, N. (1994) Smart contracts. University of Amsterdam. Available from https://www.fon.hum.uva.nl/ rob/Courses/InformationInSpeech/CDROM/Literature/ LOTwinterschool2006/szabo.best.vwh.net/smart.contracts. html

Ticketmaster (2023) Ticketmaster launches token-gated sales, enabling artists to reward fans with prioritized ticket access and concert experiences through NFTs. Available from https:// business.ticketmaster.com/business-solutions/nft-token-gated-sales

Tkachenko, A. (2022) Tokenized commodities are the safety net crypto investors always needed. Nasdaq. Available from https://www.nasdaq.com/articles/tokenized-commodities-are-the-safety-net-crypto-investors-always-needed

UNHCR (2022) UNHCR launches pilot Cash-Based Intervention using Blockchain technology for humanitarian payments to people displaced and impacted by the war in Ukraine. Available from https://www.unhcr.org/ua/en/52555-unhcr-launches-pilot-cash-based-intervention-using-blockchain-technology-for-humanitarian-payments-to-people-displaced-and-impacted-by-the-war-in-ukraine-unhcr-has-launched-a-first-of-its-kind-integ.html

US Department of Justice (2022) Justice Department announces first director of National Cryptocurrency Enforcement Team. Available from https://www.justice.gov/opa/pr/justice-department-announces-first-director-national-cryptocurrency-enforcement-team

US Department of Justice (2023) Binance and CEO plead guilty to federal charges in $4B resolution. Available from https://www.justice.gov/opa/pr/binance-and-ceo-plead-guilty-federal-charges-4b-resolution

We are Social (2024) Digital 2024 global overview, pp.179–182. Available from https://wearesocial.com/us/blog/2024/01/digital-2024/

Wolfson, R. (2018) Maltese Parliament passes laws that set regulatory framework for blockchain, cryptocurrency and DLT. Forbes. Available from https://www.forbes.com/sites/rachelwolfson/2018/07/05/maltese-parliament-passes-laws-that-set-regulatory-framework-for-blockchain-cryptocurrency-and-dlt/#7d579a9249ed

WEF (World Economic Forum) (2023) DAOs for impact. Available from https://www3.weforum.org/docs/WEF_DAOs_for_Impact_2023.pdf

World Mobile (2023) World Mobile smart village case study. Available from https://worldmobile.io/en/smartvillage

Young, M. (2023) DAO treasuries top $25 billion for the first time: DeepDAO. CoinTelegraph. Available from https://cointelegraph.com/news/dao-treasuries-top-25-billion-for-the-first-time-deepdao

Zhao, W. (2018) Japan Warns Binance exchange over licensing. CoinDesk. Available from https://www.coindesk.com/markets/2018/03/23/japan-warns-binance-exchange-over-licensing/

Published by BCS Learning & Development Ltd, a wholly owned subsidiary of BCS, The Chartered Institute for IT, 3 Newbridge Square, Swindon, SN1 1BY, UK.
www.bcs.org

Paperback ISBN: 978-1-78017-6451
PDF ISBN: 978-1-78017-6468
ePUB ISBN: 978-1-78017-6475

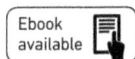

Ebook available

British Cataloguing in Publication Data.
A CIP catalogue record for this book is available at the British Library.

Publisher's acknowledgements
Reviewers: Mark Cook and Lisa Wilson
Publisher: Ian Borthwick
Commissioning editor: Heather Wood
Production manager: Florence Leroy
Project manager: Just Content
Copy-editor: Tracey Cowell
Proofreader: Susan Lyons
Cover design: Alex Wright
Cover image: istock/StationaryTraveller
Sales director: Charles Rumball
Typeset by Lapiz Digital Services, Chennai, India

BCS, THE CHARTERED INSTITUTE FOR IT

BCS, The Chartered Institute for IT, is committed to making IT good for society. We use the power of our network to bring about positive, tangible change. We champion the global IT profession and the interests of individuals, engaged in that profession, for the benefit of all.

Exchanging IT expertise and knowledge
The Institute fosters links between experts from industry, academia and business to promote new thinking, education and knowledge sharing.

Supporting practitioners
Through continuing professional development and a series of respected IT qualifications, the Institute seeks to promote professional practice tuned to the demands of business. It provides practical support and information services to its members and volunteer communities around the world.

Setting standards and frameworks
The Institute collaborates with government, industry and relevant bodies to establish good working practices, codes of conduct, skills frameworks and common standards. It also offers a range of consultancy services to employers to help them adopt best practice.

Become a member
Over 70,000 people including students, teachers, professionals and practitioners enjoy the benefits of BCS membership. These include access to an international community, invitations to a roster of local and national events, career development tools and a quarterly thought-leadership magazine. Visit www.bcs.org/membership to find out more.

Learn more about BCS qualifications and certifications at https://certifications.bcs.org/

Further information
BCS, The Chartered Institute for IT,
3 Newbridge Square, Swindon, SN1 1BY, UK.
T +44 (0) 1793 417 417
(Monday to Friday, 09:00 to 17:00 UK time)
www.bcs.org/contact
http://shop.bcs.org/

www.ingramcontent.com/pod-product-compliance
Lightning Source LLC
Chambersburg PA
CBHW042118190326
41519CB00030B/7536